UNCLE JACK'S
OUTER BANKS

By

Jack Sandberg

ISBN Number 1-57087-401-8

Professional Press
Chapel Hill, NC 27515-4371

Manufactured in the United States of America
02 01 00 99 98 97 10 9 8 7 6 5 4 3 2 1

Foreword

This book consists of a choice few of the over 450 humorous columns "Uncle Jack" has written for the **Outer Banks Sentinel** and its predecessor, the **Outer Banks Current**, weekly newspapers published in Nags Head, N.C.

Alert readers of his two previous collections may note that some of the pieces in this book are at least vaguely familiar. He assumes that the staples in those booklets have rusted out by now and the only way to preserve his better stuff for posterity is to reprint it in this more durable form.

For new readers he should explain that the ubiquitous "Mrs. Stonebreaker" in these pages is a composite of all those long-suffering teachers who tried unsuccessfully to teach him how to work those vitally important problems where two trains start out from different parts of the country and eventually meet head-on, usually somewhere in Kansas. "The Reverend Hokum" (real name Houkom) was the minister of Uncle Jack's childhood Lutheran church whose teachings he has spent a lifetime pondering, often in dismay.

The author would like to thank his terrific wife, Sue, who made this book possible by getting him out of bed in the morning and propping him up in front of his computer. Thanks also to his talented friend Mike Lucas who designed the cover, and to the dozens of patient technicians at the Gateway Computer Company in South Dakota who kept Uncle Jack's new laptop humming throughout this project.

Uncle Jack's Mailbag

Dear Uncle Jack,

On the Outer Banks, what's the difference between a "native" and a "local"?

Tourist
Pittsburgh

Dear Tourist,

A local is somebody who lives here all year round but isn't a native. Most locals used to live in or near Pittsburgh. Locals are permitted to leave the Outer Banks for up to three weeks during January or February. If they stay away longer they are shunned by other locals who sneer at them and call them tourists.

A native is somebody whose family has always lived here. Natives never leave the Outer Banks except to join the Coast Guard.

Natives converse with each other in an unintelligible tongue which linguists believe to be an early form of English. Many natives carry on the ancient trades and crafts of their forefathers such as hunting, fishing, crabbing and selling real estate.

As far as Uncle Jack has been able to determine there are no important anatomical differences between natives and locals that would prevent them from mating.

Insouciantly,

Uncle Jack

Advice for Houseguests

Uncle Jack has lived on the Outer Banks for a long time now and he has noticed some very interesting things about the flora and fauna. One thing he has noticed is that there are lots of swans around here in the winter but hardly any in the summer.

Another thing he has noticed is that houseguests are just the opposite of swans. You hardly ever see a houseguest around here in the winter but they are all over the place in the summer. Come to think of it Uncle Jack has never seen a houseguest and a swan at the same time.

Uncle Jack has noticed that the average houseguest tends to be a lot more trouble than the average swan. Swans eat out most of the time for one thing, and they never take showers. Houseguests spend most of their time sitting around the dining room table waiting for food to appear when they are not in the bathroom.

Anyway Uncle Jack thought it would be a good idea to give some advice to houseguests who are planning to come to the Outer Banks. These suggestions are not "cast in concrete" as they say over at Coastal Redi-Mix. Not everybody likes Stilton cheese, for instance, so you might not have to bring any if you are not staying with Uncle Jack.

What to bring your host and hostess:

One half-gallon Rebel Yell bourbon per person (excluding children under 5), three cases Rolling Rock beer, six pounds medium shrimp (heads off, please), two dozen steamed jumbo jimmy crabs, two dozen clams, five pounds scallops, three dozen Silver Queen corn, one bushel Currituck peaches, three pounds Stilton cheese, two cases good imported red table wine (ditto white), two loaves French bread, five pounds Virginia Diner peanuts.

Also bring assorted non-perishable items such as canned truffles and caviar that your host and hostess can enjoy next winter while watching the swans.

Also bring sheets, pillow cases, towels, soap, deodorant, toothpaste, shampoo, depilatories, aspirin, insect spray, styrofoam coolers and good books, all of which you should remember to forget when you leave.

Chores your host and hostess should not have to do during your visit: Cook meals, wash dishes, take out garbage, clean bathtub, scratch dogs, mow lawn, make morning coffee, smile.

Things you can do to express appreciation to your host and hostess: Go to see **The Lost Colony** every night by yourselves. Talk about pleasant things like what you are planning to fix for dinner tomorrow night or where you are planning to take your host and hostess for lunch. Do not talk about the horrible traffic or how the developers are ruining the Outer Banks or how rotten the fishing is in the summer or how terrible the weather has been during your visit.

Your host and hostess do not want to have to tell you how wonderful the weather was last week, how great the fishing is in the spring and fall, or how easy it is to cross the Bypass in February.

If you do everything Uncle Jack has suggested your host and hostess might invite you to come back again. If you are really lucky they might ask you to come back next winter when the swans are here.

Shredded Hopes

Dear Uncle Jack,

I spent two weeks on the Outer Banks last summer and now I spend most of my time trying to figure out how I could make a living down there. I have a terrific job running a shredding machine for the C.I.A. and I'm really good at it so I was wondering if you knew anybody down there who is looking for an experienced shredder. I could be there tomorrow if they need me and if the hours were right I would even consider working for less than the $75,000 I'm making now. I won't sleep until I hear from you, Uncle Jack, so please hurry.

Anxious
McLean, Virginia

Dear Anxious,

Uncle Jack is certainly glad to hear that you would be willing to take a modest pay cut because that will help you a lot when you go looking for a job down here. He is not sure what they are paying paper shredders over at the county office building but he doubts if it's anywhere near $75,000. They have surprised him before, though, so you might want to check it out when you get down here.

The big problem you face, though, is that there just aren't that many openings for paper shredders down here due to the general lack of large scale covert activity. There is probably a little hanky panky from time to time in some of the lawyers' offices but most of it usually gets torn up by hand and flushed down the toilet.

What it boils down to if you ask Uncle Jack, and you did, is that you might have to go into some other line of work, or at least you might have to adapt your highly developed shredding skills to something other than paper.

Have you thought about cabbage? There is hardly a restaurant on the Outer Banks that doesn't have to make a ton of coleslaw every day and that means shredding a lot of cabbage. You might think about picking up a government surplus high performance shredder and setting yourself up in the wholesale coleslaw business.

If you want to know the truth that is about the only business he can think of that there is not at least two of already on the Outer Banks. For example if you are thinking about opening a discount department store forget it. There is already a Wal-Mart and a K-Mart down here and that's at least one too many if you ask Uncle Jack.

He knows how you feel about wanting to move to the Outer Banks, though, because he had the same problem once, a long time ago. All he can say is that if you want to live here badly enough you will find a way.

Optimistically,
Uncle Jack

P.S. How do you feel about selling real estate?

Court Report

Two errant motorists were brought to the bar of justice in District Court last week when Judge Fentress ("Relentless Fentress") Warmer continued his dogged campaign to rid the Outer Banks of drunk drivers before the tourist season begins.

In the morning session Miss Cindi Stupendas of Kill Devil Hills pleaded not guilty to charges of indecent exposure and driving under the influence. Officer Clyde Truthful of Nags Head testified that he was on routine patrol when he observed Miss Stupendas, a statuesque blonde, driving her silver Mercedes-Benz convertible "in a careless and erotic manner" on the Beach Road near the Sea Farm hotel at 1:45 a.m. Wednesday.

He pursued the suspect in the town's new high-mileage Suzuki Samurai patrol car but was unable to overtake the faster Mercedes until it came to a stop in the swimming pool of the Last Colony Inn. According to officer Truthful the accused was "floating real nice but too drunk to dogpaddle" when he rescued her from the pool. He further testified that he administered mouth-to-mouth resuscitation to the accused for nearly an hour before calling other rescue personnel to the scene.

Taking the stand in her own defense, Miss Stupendas, attired in a fetching gold lame stretch leotard with matching Gucci high-heeled clogs, explained to the court that on the night in question, having just left her weekly group therapy session at the home of friends in Kitty Hawk, she had noticed a smudge on the hood of her Mercedes which she foolishly attempted to remove without first stopping the car.

She surmised that it was just after her shoulder straps broke that officer Truthful had happened upon the scene, by which time she had decided to seek professional assistance in cleaning her car. While proceeding south on the Beach Road, she said, she was momentarily blinded by her own cigarette lighter and mistook the Last Colony's swimming pool for a drive-in carwash, a mistake she thought anyone could have made under the circumstances.

Miss Stupendas further testified that she had refused to take the breathalyzer test on religious grounds, explaining that the members of her faith are expressly forbidden to expend breath after midnight except in praise of their Creator.

Obviously impressed by the defendant's sincerity, contriteness and generally spectacular appearance, Judge Warmer departed somewhat from his usually stern treatment of DUI offenders. The judge, who is reported to have said once that in his considered opinion "a pretty woman is naturally incapable of committing a crime", dismissed the indecent exposure charge on grounds that he could not believe that Miss Stupendas would not look fairly decent even without a stitch on.

He did, however, caution her firmly to refrain from driving her car again until it has been removed from the Last Colony pool.

After a brief recess for lunch Judge Warmer returned to the bench for the trial of Germont Wayne "Chubby" Tubbs, 19, of Drainfield who was arraigned last week on charges of driving under the influence, resisting arrest, and unauthorized consumption of hushpuppies.

According to testimony offered by twelve area law officers who participated in Tubbs' apprehension, the youth had led them on a hair-raising, high-speed chase through Kitty Hawk, Kill Devil Hills, Nags Head, Manns Harbor and Stumpy Point before crashing his modified

1968 John Deere riding mower through the front door of Louie's Lobster Lounge on the causeway.

The arresting officers testified that Tubbs, who is five feet seven inches tall and weighs 420 pounds, held them at bay for 20 minutes while he consumed four baskets of Louie's famous hushpuppies and a quart of Fresca, after which he agreed to go quietly to the Manteo jail.

Tubbs reportedly blew an .83 on the breathalyzer which the Sheriff's department promptly submitted to the Guinness Book of Records as a new high for northern Dare County this year.

Tubbs, an unemployed scallop shucker, testified that he had no idea that anybody was chasing him because he was playing his 8-track "real loud" in order to hear a Loretta Lynn tape over the noise of his mower which he admitted probably needs a new muffler.

The defendant insisted that he had consumed only one small glass of Piesporter Reisling '68 with his dinner at the Soundfare restaurant and attributed the high breathalyzer reading to his rare medical condition called "East Lake Syndrome" which causes corn meal to turn to alcohol in his stomach.

Tubbs' court-appointed lawyer, Claiborne Prawn of Elizabeth City, called several character witnesses to the stand in an apparent effort to distract attention from his client's 37 previous convictions on charges ranging from cruelty to oysters to eating a hang glider.

Obviously unimpressed, Judge Warmer ordered the youth to surrender his driver's license or go to jail. Lawyer Prawn informed the judge that his client would be unable to surrender his license because he had eaten it last month when he mistook his wallet for a cheeseburger while dining at a local fast-food restaurant.

Tubbs said he would cheerfully go to jail if the judge would promise to assign him to kitchen duty.

Croaker Recipe

(From Uncle Jack's Outer Banks Cookbook)

One medium croaker, unscaled, head on
One cup crushed bran flakes
Three tablespoons cod liver oil
One cup crushed ice
Four ounces cognac

Roll croaker in bran flakes until well coated. Fry in cod liver oil, three minutes on each side. Remove from pan and set aside. Pour cognac over crushed ice. Drink cognac while waiting for croaker to cool. When croaker has reached room temperature, feed to cat. (Cats like croaker; Uncle Jack does not.)

Concentrated Sludge

Uncle Jack saw in the paper the other day where the Town of Manteo has a used Smith and Loveless 40" Sludge Concentrator for sale. He is not personally in the market for a sludge concentrator right now, but he thought he should pass the information along to anybody who might have missed the advertisement. You don't get an opportunity to pick up a good sludge concentrator every day, that's for sure.

If you want to know the truth, Uncle Jack is not sure what he would do with a sludge concentrator if he was lucky enough to get one. All he can think of is that it might make a nice gift for his Congressman. They are producing some serious sludge up there in Washington these days, and a good concentrator could come in handy. A 40-incher might not be big enough to do the job though, the way things are going in Congress.

Anyway, Uncle Jack is happy as a clam that the **Outer Banks Sentinel** is giving him another chance to write about drainage and sewage and erosion and pollution and all the other neglected topics that are near and dear to his heart because they contribute so much to the quality of life here on the Outer Banks. It has been eight years since he wrote his last column for the late **Outer Banks Current**, and he has to confess he has missed doing it more than he thought he would.

Uncle Jack has to tell you that the people who run this paper really know how to drive a hard bargain. They got him into Kelly's Tavern a few weeks ago and started giving him all the free beer he could drink, which is still a lot even though he is officially a senior citizen now. (Other parts of Uncle Jack's body have pretty much shriveled up in his old age, but his bladder is still amazingly supple—probably because of all the exercise it gets.) Anyway, they wouldn't let him go to the men's room until he said he would start writing his column again, so he didn't have a whole lot of choice.

Unfortunately, one part of Uncle Jack that really has shriveled up is his brain, so he is afraid he might not remember he is supposed to do this every week. He is hoping his readers will help to remind him by writing letters and asking him hard questions the way they used to in the **Current.**

As a bona fide high school graduate from back in the days when it really meant something, he is ready to tackle tough questions on just about any subject from sewage disposal to epistemology.

What he liked most about writing his column was trying to answer deep philosophical questions like "How many Realtors does it take to replace a light bulb?" and "How many politicians does it take to replace a light bulb?" Lawyers were always asking him questions like that for some reason.

Anyway Uncle Jack has been soaking his rusty old Underwood typewriter in a bucket of WD-40 and as soon as he locates a new ribbon—probably in some Third World country—he will be ready to rock and roll again.

Suddenly Last Summer

A One-Act Play Written For the Theatre of the Absurd

---

by
Pier Andello

Time: Mid-morning on an overcast Wednesday in early June, only a few days into a new tourist season.

Place: A small poster gallery and framing shop somewhere on the Outer Banks.

Characters: Uncle Jack, the kindly old proprietor
Male tourist
Female tourist
Male tourist #2
Female tourist #2

<u>Scene One</u>

UJ: Mornin' folks. Can I help.......
MT & FT (in unison): Just browsing.
UJ: Where you folks from?
MT: Ahia
UJ: Wow! What part of Ahia?
MT: Up by Canton.
UJ: Ah yes. Canton. Home of the Bulldogs.
MT: Huh?

UJ: Bulldogs. Used to be a famous football team.
MT: Musta been before my time.
UJ: I used to live in Pittsburgh which is right up by Ohio.
MT: No kidding. I used to have a cousin lived in Pittsburgh.
UJ: It's a small world, that's for sure. Your first visit to the Outer Banks?
MT: Nope. Been comin' down here for 25 years.
UJ: Wow. You must like it down here.
MT: Used to like it a lot more. Too many people down here now. They're wreckin' the place.
UJ: Who's wreckin' the place?
MT: All them developers. They ought to string 'em up.
UJ: (after driving #3 finishing nail into left index finger) Damn!
FT: There ought to be a law against all this building.
UJ: (Sagely) It's a free country you know. You can't stop people from building on their own property.
MT: Well you better do something before it's too late. Nobody from Ahia is gonna wanna come down here anymore if you keep this up.
UJ: (Sagely) Well it's still not half as bad as a lot of other places and besides, all these new stores and everything mean jobs for a lot of people. I'll bet if all this growth was happening up in Canton a lot of people would be happy about it.
MT: (Looks away in disgust as Uncle Jack neatly slices off tip of left index finger with mat knife) I don't care. We came down here to get away from all the noise and traffic and people and now it's all down here, too.
UJ: (Sagely) Well you might as well try to get used to it and enjoy yourselves because there is nothing you or anybody else can do about it and it's going to keep on like this right up to the next bad hurricane and then it

will start all over again.
MT: Well, Myrt. See anything you like?
FT: (Brandishing swatch of maroon naugahyde) Can't find anything that goes with the couch. You got any other art galleries around here might have a seascape with some maroon in it?
UJ: You could try Wal-Mart.
MT: Nice talkin' to you son. You take care of that finger and look us up if you ever get to Canton.
UJ: Y'all come back now, hear?

Scene Two

Time: Ten minutes later.

UJ: Mornin' folks. Can I help........
MT2 & FT2: (in unison) Just browsing.
UJ: Where you folks from?
MT2: Ahia.
UJ: (After dropping crate of glass on foot) Damn!

Curtain

Outer Banks Trivia

Uncle Jack has spent a fair amount of his life trying to figure out some way to get rich and famous without working but he has not come up with anything yet and sometimes he wonders if he ever will. He is not a quitter though so he keeps trying to think of something at all times and he usually manages to stay fairly cheerful even though he is still poor and unknown.

The only time Uncle Jack gets a little depressed is when he hears about how some other person has come up with a terrific money-making idea he should have thought of himself and how that person is getting filthy rich.

This happened to him last week when he read in the paper about this man who invented a new game called **College Trivia** or something like that which is just like **Trivial Pursuit** except that all the questions are just like the questions they put in the **SAT Test** which is what all the high school graduates take if they want to get into college.

Uncle Jack is a high school graduate as he might have mentioned once or twice before and he remembers how he had to take that test and how hard the questions were and how nice it would be if you could study up for it before you took it.

It is a very hard test to study for, though, because the questions are fairly dumb for the most part and you tend to fall asleep before you get very far into your studying and that is why it was so smart for that man to put it into the form of a game.

People will enjoy almost anything if you make a game out of it and that is why even something as stupid as football has caught on and is now quite popular in some circles. The same thing is happening with the **SAT Test** game which is making several people very rich and Uncle Jack very jealous.

Like he said before, though, he never gives up and it did not take him very long to come up with a new game which he is calling **Outer Banks Trivia** and he is hoping it will catch on enough so he can make a down payment on a new secondhand Jeep or maybe even a Hummer.

So far he has only had time to think of a few questions for his new game but maybe they will give you some idea of how it will go:

1. Manteo is
a. more often mispronounced by tourists than Rodanthe.
b. less often mispronounced by tourists than Wanchese.
c. more often mispronounced by tourists than Bodie Island.
d. less often mispronounced by tourists than Duck.
e. more often ducked by tourists than mispronounced.

2. Chicamacomico is
a. the way a few people spell Chicamacomico.
b. Colonel Sanders' favorite vacation spot.
c. an Indian word meaning "two feet of water covering Highway 12."
d. what they used to call Avon before they found out that "Chicamacomico" was too long to fit over the door of the new post office.

3. Which of the following best describes the town of Southern Shores?
a. "Gateway to Duck."
b. "Nine Holes and a Nap."

c. "Pentagon-by-the-Sea."
d. "The Outer Banks best-planned, best-governed and most beautiful residential community."

4. Nags Head is to Kill Devil Hills as
a. Salvo is to Waves.
b. Buxton is to Avon.
c. Hatteras Village is to Frisco.
d. Southern Shores is to Sodom and Gomorrah.
e. all of the above.

5. "Development" is to "Outer Banks" as
a. fertilizer is to flowers.
b. rape is to virgin.
c. McDonalds is to ground beef.
d. H-bomb is to Hiroshima.

Anyway that's the way Uncle Jack's **Outer Banks Trivia** game will go and he will be happy to get lots of contributions from his readers so he does not have to do all the hard thinking himself. And if he does finally get rich he promises to spread his wealth around, too, especially in the bars and restaurants.

Hatteras Lite

Dear Uncle Jack,

I have to tell you I am really tired of hearing about the Hatteras lighthouse. What is such a big deal about lighthouses anyway? Nobody needs them anymore since they invented radar and sonar and all that stuff so why spend a lot of money trying to keep a lighthouse from falling down when there are so many other things that we really need like an elevated highway from Oregon Inlet to Buxton?

You're pretty smart, Uncle Jack, so I presume you agree with me that they ought to let the lighthouse fall in the drink but I wouldn't be surprised if you were too chicken to come right out and admit it in public.

Len Fresnel
Avon

Dear Len,

First of all Uncle Jack would like to say that if he thought it would be best to let the lighthouse fall in the ocean he would come right out and say it. He is not running for office so there is no reason for him to lie about what he really thinks.

Right now he is leaning toward letting it fall in the ocean, primarily because it would be so much fun to watch on TV. Uncle Jack has seen those movies on TV where they put a lot of dynamite in a building and blow it up and the whole thing falls down in a big heap of rubble and he never fails to get a big kick out of watching that, especially when they do it in slow motion about six times. He can hardly imagine what a thrill it would be to watch that lighthouse fall into the ocean due to natural causes without the use of any artificial substances such as dynamite.

Uncle Jack is pretty sure that an event like this would get terrific ratings on the TV and if the people in charge of the lighthouse played their cards right they could make enough money out of it to build a much nicer, higher lighthouse with all the amenities such as jacuzzis and elevators and skyboxes where the big corporations could entertain politicians and other important people and write it off as a business expense.

If Uncle Jack was in charge he would start right away to put out a line of T-shirts each one of which would have a day, hour and minute printed on it and the proceeds would go into a big pool and the person who has the closest time to when the lighthouse falls down would win a nice prize like breakfast at Sam and Omie's and the rest of the money would go toward building a bigger and better lighthouse in a safer place like over behind the reverse osmosis plant.

The present lighthouse is not the first one at Hatteras or even the second so it is not as though something like this has never happened before. Each succeeding lighthouse has been bigger and better than the one before and there is no reason this could not be the case again. Everybody would have to watch out to make sure the contractors did not try to build it out of particle board but that does not seem like an insurmountable problem.

Uncle Jack has many more ideas about how to deal with the lighthouse quandary but he is running out of space and will have to save them for the future, assuming there is one.

Optimistically,
Uncle Jack

Social Notes From the Mainland

Mrs. Carter Fry hosted the Grumpy Harbor Ladies Literary Society at her home on Route 6 last Thursday. Luncheon was served followed by election of officers and a dramatic reading by Mrs. Otho Scramm of selections from the current best-selling novel **Hot Mountain**. Mrs. Delmore Wiggett fainted during the reading and had to be rushed to the clinic in Manteo where she remained in intensive care for several hours.

Mr. Carter Fry went to Plymouth on Thursday and has not returned.

Miss LuWanda Crammitt, daughter of Mrs. Opal Crammitt of Clamflats, has a speaking part in a new feature film entitled **Debbie Does Amsterdam**, the latest release in the highly acclaimed **Debbie** series of travelogues from Mammary Studios. LuWanda, who is known professionally as Debbie Craven, is employed as a masseuse in Los Angeles, California while pursuing her acting career. She was a 1992 graduate of Thassamusketo High School where she was voted "Most Likely To" by the boys of the senior class.

Mr. Albert Zebulon, manager of the Grumpy Harbor 6-12 convenience store, was in Nags Head last week attending an Executive Training Conference at the Ramada Inn. More than 300 managers of 6-12 stores in the three-county Eastern Swamps Division attended the meeting which focused on helping convenience store managers cope with inflation. Mr. Zebulon attended seminars on "How to Squeeze 50 Extra Cups from Each Pound of Coffee," "Save $$$ by Recycling Used Stirring Sticks" and "Creative Bookkeeping."

Mrs. Estelle Jones went to the HMO in Columbia on Monday to have her corns pared.

Billy Frank Weddle, son of Mr. and Mrs. Jimmy Joe Weddle of Drainfield, was home last week on a three-day pass from the East Carolina Correctional Center in Clam Quarter where he recently starred in an inmate production of Verdi's "La Forza del Destino."

Mrs. Greb Fillett and Mrs. Nettie Clayford drove to Norfolk on Wednesday in Mrs. Clayford's new Ford Siesta with optional overdrive. They got 43.6 miles to the gallon according to Mrs. Clayford's daughter Lula who is home on vacation from Central Junior Bible College in Charlotte where she is majoring in long division.

Fardley Place

Located on the Dare County mainland, not far from the picturesque village of Drainfield, Fardley Place is believed by local historians to be the site of the first permanent mobile home residence in the United States.

According to records in the archives of the N.C. Department of Transportation, the Alpheus Fardley family of Nutley, New Jersey were en route to Florida in search of work when a flat tire on their "house trailer", as such vehicles were called in those days, brought their journey to a premature end on December 18, 1928.

Unable to afford a tire patch, the penurious Fardleys were forced to remain parked on the shoulder of state highway 263 for several months, subsisting primarily on the remains of turtles and possums whose carcasses litter the roads in that area.

Eventually the luckless travelers were befriended by a group of moderately xenophobic local residents who helped them move their trailer to a vacant field nearby. Once settled the industrious Fardleys quickly found steady employment as scallop shuckers and in a few short years were able to replace their tiny domicile with a six-room, state-of-the-art, Conner "Palais de Versailles" model with indoor facilities.

The family remained in residence at Fardley Place until December 1941 when "opportunity knocked" in the form of the Japanese sneak attack on Pearl Harbor. The senior Fardleys and their nine children promptly moved to the Norfolk area where they reportedly amassed a considerable fortune in shipbuilding, real estate, and fried chicken during World War II.

While no trace remains of the Fardley trailer, which was reportedly blown to a new location in Tyrrell County during Hurricane Hazel in 1954, the cement blocks on which it stood are still clearly visible at low tide. The Fardley yard, however, has been preserved intact as a living museum of depression-era North Caroliniana.

Visitors may view (and children may climb on!) the remains of no fewer than 20 assorted Ford and Chevrolet vehicles (circa 1926-38) which the Fardleys acquired and discarded during their 13 years in Dare County.

Four partially collapsed sheds on the property shelter the rusting remnants of one of the most comprehensive collections of broken farm implements and household appliances ever assembled by a single family east of the Mississippi.

Lovingly cultivated by the ladies of the Drainfield Garden Club, the Fardley Yard also contains one of the largest displays of indigenous weeds in eastern North Carolina.

Fardley Place is open to the public every day and admission is free. From Nags Head drive west on highway 263 to Drainfield. Turn around at the Methodist Church and drive back exactly 1.2 miles. Look for the miniature replica of Stonehenge cleverly fashioned out of cement blocks by the Men's Auxiliary of the Drainfield Garden Club.

Rassling for Dollars

Uncle Jack has been kicking himself all week because he missed what was probably the premiere cultural event of the season in Dare County last Friday night. He wasted the whole evening watching the **Hornets** beat the **Knicks** when he could have been down at the Hatteras High School gym watching the traveling troupe of musclebound thespians known as **Wrestlemania** put on their show.

Uncle Jack has seen a fair amount of rassling on the TV over the years which he has watched in utter amazement but he has never had a chance to watch live rasslers at work in their chosen profession; kicking, stomping, gouging, pulling hair, head-butting, smashing their opponents to the floor and jumping up and down on them and so on. He really wanted to find out how they can do these things without hurting each other and getting mad.

Uncle Jack was thinking that if he could find out how the rasslers do what they do to each other and then manage to get back on the same bus together that maybe he could find a clue as to how to bring about peace between the Arabs and the Israelis.

Uncle Jack also saw in the paper where they were going to have a special "Dog Food" match where the winner would get $500 and the loser would have to eat a can of dog food. He could not help thinking what a big step forward this is civilization-wise from when the Romans would put a Christian in the ring with a lion and more often than not the Christian would wind up as cat food.

Anyway Uncle Jack is sorry he missed the whole thing because he is sure that **Wrestlemania** was a terrifically educational experience for all the children of Hatteras Island, especially the ones under ten years old who could get in for only $5.00. If you ask him the way things are going in the world these days grown-ups who are really good at kicking and gouging and head-butting are probably about the best role models you can find for the young people.

It said in the paper that proceeds from the rassling show would benefit the junior class at Cape Hatteras High School which sure beats washing cars as a character-builder if you ask Uncle Jack. Maybe they could use the money for a field trip to some uplifting place like Las Vegas.

Anyway you can be sure that if **Wrestlemania** comes back to Hatteras High School next year Uncle Jack will be there—unless, of course, the county commissioners happen to be meeting the same night. When it comes to fighting he would much rather watch the real thing anytime.

Drilling for Dollars

Dear Uncle Jack,

I read in the paper where the Chevron oil company wants to drill for oil about 40 miles out in the ocean off Hatteras. They say there is hardly any chance they will find anything but they are willing to spend a few million dollars to find out. Are those people nuts or what, Uncle Jack?

Incredulous
Avon

Dear Incredulous,

When he first read about this plan to drill for oil out in the ocean Uncle Jack thought it was pretty crazy, too, but then he started thinking about the other places they have gone looking for oil and it didn't seem so strange anymore.

For one thing they found oil way up in the northern part of Alaska by the Arctic Circle and then they had to build a pipeline about a thousand miles long to carry it down to the nearest seaport which was a little fishing village called Valdez which you may remember reading about a couple of years ago when the tanker ran aground and spilled a zillion gallons of Valdez oil into the ocean up there.

Drilling a well off Hatteras would be a piece of cake compared to drilling wells on the Arctic Circle and if they did find oil they would only need a 40-mile long pipeline to pump it into the nearest fishing village. With a little bad luck Wanchese could be just as famous as Valdez some day.

If you ask Uncle Jack you have to give the oil companies credit for what they are trying to do which is to reduce America's dependence on foreign oil. It is very scary to think that something like 70% of all the oil we burn up in our cars and trucks and airplanes—and most important our 4WD recreational vehicles—comes from unstable places like the Middle East and South America and Africa.

It is entirely possible that if Chevron brings in a big gusher or two out by the Gulf Stream, America could reduce its dependence on foreign oil from 70% to maybe 69% for a couple of years before it runs out and they have to drill someplace else—like maybe off the end of Jennette's pier. By that time there could be so much oil on the beaches around here that nobody would care.

Anyway Uncle Jack is glad that there are selfless, patriotic oil companies like Chevron who are willing to risk millions of dollars in what could well be a futile effort to free us from the specter of oil deprivation at the hands of greedy middle eastern potentates, some of whom probably do not even believe in the Bible.

Even so, he hopes they do not get permission to drill their well and if they do he hopes it is a dry hole if such a thing is possible out by the Gulf Stream. He has confidence that our many armed forces which will cost about $250 billion to maintain this year alone, will keep that foreign oil flowing no matter what. What else could possibly justify spending that much money on "defense" when there isn't anybody left to defend against?

Testily,
Uncle Jack

Ice Plant Island

Dear Uncle Jack,

I read in the paper where they are trying to think up a new name for Ice Plant Island which would make it sound classier for the tourists. Some people want to call it New World Park and other people want to call it Roanoke Festival Park and other people want to name it after Wanchese or Manteo or some of the other natives who lived around here in the old days before the first outlet mall.

I know you have probably thought about this a lot yourself, Uncle Jack, so I would like to know what you think they should call it.

Common Mann
Mann's Harbor

Dear Common,

The guiding principle of Uncle Jack's life so far has been "do whatever is easiest" and this is the main reason why he thinks they should just leave it Ice Plant Island. Everybody who lives around here knows where Ice Plant Island is so if they are in a good mood they can tell the tourists how to get there.

If they change the name to something fancy like Roanoke Festival Park nobody is going to know what the tourists are talking about when they ask for directions and they could all end up over at the landfill or somewhere.

Also Ice Plant Island is something just about everybody can pronounce correctly even if they are from Ahia or New Jersey. The tourists have enough trouble already with names like Wanchese and Manteo and Chicamacomico and Bodie Island without creating another problem for them.

Uncle Jack thinks the tourists should be able to enjoy their vacations without having to worry about how to pronounce something every time they turn around.

Also Uncle Jack has never heard of any other place in the world that has an Ice Plant Island and as far as he is concerned that should be enough reason not to change it. "Ireland" probably sounded like a pretty dumb name for an island at one time but the Irish people stuck to it and now many people from all over the world like to go there on their vacations. If you ask Uncle Jack there is a lesson there for all of us.

Conservatively,
Uncle Jack

Dictionary of Outer Banks Medical Terms

BARIUM—What you do when CPR fails.

HERPES—The wife's vegetables.

DILATE—To have lived a full life.

MORBID—A higher offer.

TUMOR—An extra pair.

BENIGN—After you be eight.

Let Her Lie

Uncle Jack has a good friend named O'Brien who lives up in New Jersey where you can get the **New York Times** delivered every day if you want to. This has never seemed to Uncle Jack to be a good enough reason to live in New Jersey but O'Brien seems to think it is and Uncle Jack is glad about that because whenever an article about the Outer Banks appears in the **New York Times** O'Brien clips it out and sends it to him.

This is good because the **New York Times** tells you everything you could possibly want to know about something and then some and you always get a fresh perspective on the subject no matter how much you thought you knew about it. This week O'Brien sent a clipping about the wreck of the Civil War ship called the **Monitor** which sank in a storm off Hatteras at the very end of 1862, one hundred and thirty five years ago.

The reason the **New York Times** is writing about the **Monitor** now is that various "experts" are saying it is now or never if we want to try to salvage the wreckage and get it into a museum someplace where people can stare at it in comfort instead of risking their lives to dive down 230 feet in a rubber suit to stare at it.

The experts say it would cost about $50 million to bring up all the pieces that are left but it would only cost about $22 million to bring up the propellor and the turret which are about the only things recognizable after 130 years of damage from saltwater and fishermen's nets and maybe even a depth charge or two during World War II.

Uncle Jack was in the navy and he knows that with the sonar they had in those days it would be easy to mistake the wreck of the **Monitor** for a German submarine or even a large tuna.

Anyway it is not easy to raise $50 million or even $22 million to do something that is not going to make a lot of money for somebody so the people who want to salvage the wreckage are trying to make the **Monitor** sound like it is the most important ship ever built and that it would be a crime against civilization not to spend a paltry $22 million or whatever to haul it up.

One man who wrote a book about the **Monitor** went so far as to say that when it comes to being important the **Monitor** is "on the level with the Wright Brothers' airplane" which is funny enough to make Uncle Jack wonder if he shouldn't be the main speaker at the next meeting of the Man Will Never Fly Society. This same author suggests that maybe the U.S. Navy should put up most of the money because of its pride in its "high tech history" which suggests to Uncle Jack that he doesn't know as much about the navy as he should.

Uncle Jack spent most of his waking hours while he was in the navy reading Samuel Eliot Morison's **History of U.S. Naval Operations in World War II** from which he concluded that the less said about "high-tech operations" the better—including dropping depth charges on the **Monitor** which was perfectly capable of falling apart without any help from the Navy.

If you ask Uncle Jack it would be better to let sleeping turrets lie and spend the money on something really worthwhile like moving the Hatteras Lighthouse to the moon, and eventually to Mars if the Park Service can scrape up the money.

Lottery Losers

Dear Uncle Jack,

I read in the paper that some of the politicians in Raleigh think it would be a good idea to have a North Carolina lottery just like they have up in Virginia. They say it would keep North Carolina people from having to go up to Virginia to buy their lottery tickets and also it would help to raise money for charities such as the schools and old people.

I don't personally plan to waste so much as a dime on lottery tickets so it sounds like a pretty good idea to me, especially if they raise enough money off the gamblers to lower my taxes. Also I am pretty old, just like you, so maybe we could both get something out of it.

What do you think, Uncle Jack?

Aging Pragmatist
Southern Shores

Dear Aging,

Uncle Jack is glad you asked him about the lottery because he has been thinking a lot about it lately. He also read in the paper where some of the politicians want to have a referendum on the lottery which is how they can find out what the voters think first before they make up their own minds about the lottery. If the voters are for the lottery then they can safely vote for the lottery, too. This is not exactly what you could call "leadership" but it gets the job done sometimes.

If you want to know the truth Uncle Jack thinks state-operated lotteries stink. They had one in Pennsylvania when he lived there and they had one in Virginia when he lived there so he knows how they work. The way they work is to try to make people think they have a good chance to solve all their problems by buying lottery tickets but if that doesn't work out which it almost never does at least the losers can feel like they are contributing to a worthy cause.

Uncle Jack does not think that the state government should tell lies to people to get them to spend their money on lottery tickets. Individual politicians tell the people enough lies already without the whole government doing it, too.

He thinks that people should be allowed to gamble if they want to because they are going to anyway but if you ask him the government should be trying to talk people out of gambling not into gambling.

Uncle Jack does not think gambling is necessarily immoral or evil or anything like that and neither does the Pope as far as he can tell or he would not allow all those Bingo games in the church social halls. And he is not about to say that the Lions Club should stop leading people astray with their Bingo games, either, because nobody who plays Bingo is laboring under the delusion that winning a stuffed bunny is going to magically solve all their problems.

What is immoral is for the state government to try to suck poor people into spending what little money they have on pipe dreams with 7 million to 1 odds. If you ask Uncle Jack one of the saddest sights you can see is the lines of poor people waiting to buy lottery tickets in the convenience stores up in Virginia.

Why any self-respecting politician would want to bring that pitiful sight to all of North Carolina is beyond Uncle Jack's understanding.

All Things Considered

Dear Uncle Jack,

I am proud to say that I am a high school graduate just like yourself but I am not the kind of person who sits around on her laurels. I am constantly trying to make myself a more refined and classy type of person so I will always feel comfortable in any social situation I might get into on the Outer Banks.

Every week I read **Parade** and **People** cover to cover so when I go to a pig pickin' or an oyster roast I can talk intelligently about world affairs.

I know enough to serve red wine with Big Macs and white wine with grits and I also know that Grand Marnier over vanilla yogurt makes a very nice quick dessert.

Every time I go to the Seamark I buy a different kind of lettuce and I am trying very hard to learn the names of all the unusual vegetables they have over there.

So you can see, Uncle Jack, that I am doing my best to make my home a small oasis of elegance and refinement in the midst of the cultural desert in which we live here on the Outer Banks.

This is a lot harder to do than it was in Akron, though, and one of the main reasons is the radio. Up in Akron I could perform my housewifely duties in a much more refined and dignified manner because I could listen to beautiful music by such well-known composers as Bach, Beethoven and Buxtehude which they played at all times on the National Public Radio station. You can believe me when I tell you, Uncle Jack, that I miss that radio station more than anything else I left behind in Akron including my husband and six children and I think the Outer Banks would be a much better place for high school graduates to live if we had one like it.

Why don't we have one like it, Uncle Jack?

Culture Vulture
Kitty Hawk

Dear Vulture,

Uncle Jack is very glad you wrote because he feels exactly the way you do. One of the nicest things about New Orleans where he spends a lot of time is the two public radio stations they have where you can listen to classical music and good jazz and excellent news programs at any time of the day and night without commercials.

Unfortunately he cannot tell you why we do not have a PBS radio station to listen to on the Outer Banks because he does not know. He has never understood why everybody else in North Carolina should have a PBS station to listen to but not us. We are not all lepers over here, after all.

Uncle Jack is willing to bet that if our state senator had been on the Radio Commission all those years instead of the Highway Commission we would have a PBS station to listen to by now instead of all those bike paths we have all over the place but that is not the way it worked out.

He is hoping that some day we will have one but in the meantime he will just have to keep riding his bike.

Hopefully,
Uncle Jack

You Might Be a Teacher

Uncle Jack has a friend named Roy who lives out in cyberspace somewhere and from time to time sends him funny things by e-mail which he calls "column fodder". It is nice to have a friend like Roy when you have to write a column every week and you feel like you are essentially brain dead when the time comes to do it.

This week Roy sent a piece called **You Might Be a Teacher If....** which is pretty dark humor but as an ex-teacher Uncle Jack can tell you it has the ring of truth so he is going to pass along a few excerpts:

YOU MIGHT BE A TEACHER IF......

* you believe that the staff room should have a valium saltlick.

* you can tell it's a full moon without ever looking outside.

* marking all A's on the report card would make your life SO much simpler.

* you believe in the aerial spraying of Prozac.

* you encourage obnoxious parents to look into charter schools or home schooling.

* you wonder how some parents managed to reproduce.

And it goes on in that jocular vein for another page or two which Uncle Jack would be happy to e-mail to any teacher who wants to post it in the teachers' room next to the vending machine which is no substitute for a valium salt lick but it's all most teachers have.

Speaking of vending machines Uncle Jack read in the paper this week that the Wake County schools over by Raleigh are thinking about making a deal with a soft drink company whereby the company would give the schools a ton of money to buy computers and whatever if the schools would agree to promote the company's products in the schools.

If they signed up with Coca-Cola they would sell only Coca-Cola products in the vending machines and they would have Coca-Cola ads on the school buses and maybe even the teachers would have little Coke logos tattooed on their foreheads.

If you think this is the dumbest idea you have ever heard of and you think it could never happen Uncle Jack can tell you it has already happened in Texas which is usually second to California when it comes to bizarre behavior but appears to be clearly out in front on this one.

And if you think it couldn't happen in the Gret Stet of North Carolina Uncle Jack can only quote the superintendent of the Wake County schools who says, "You test where a community would want to be on this, of course. But I promise you this sort of thing is coming."

Visionary thinkers like Uncle Jack would foresee a happy day ahead when schools no longer have to beg for money from politicians who are driven primarily by the need to keep property taxes down and thereby ensure their re-election.

Why not fund schools entirely out of advertising revenues? "Get 'em while they're young" has been an axiom of advertising from day one so why not capitalize on it? Sell the schools to the highest bidders in every category from aardvarks to zircons and watch the money roll in.

And where could the public schools find a better role model than the great University of North Carolina, a.k.a. Nike U.?

Not All Bad

Dear Uncle Jack,

Next week I start my first job as a schoolteacher and I'm really looking forward to it because I love children and I want to do good things that will make the world a better place to live in. But I am also a little bit scared and I know you used to be a teacher so I was wondering if you had any good advice for a beginner.

Nervous Nellie
New Jersey

Dear Nellie,

It is too late for Uncle Jack to give you the advice he always gives young people who want to be schoolteachers which is the same advice his Aunt Esther used to give him back when he wanted to be a teacher which was "Forget it."

But even if it was not too late and he did give you that advice you would probably not pay any attention just like Uncle Jack did not pay any attention to his Aunt Esther even though he knew that she knew an awful lot about schoolteaching after doing it for 30 years.

Anyway you sound like the kind of person who has not gone into schoolteaching just for the money and prestige so Uncle Jack is glad he did not have a chance to talk you out of it. Somebody has to teach the children so it might as well be persons like yourself who actually like children and want to make the world a better place for them instead of witches like his old fourth grade teacher, Mrs. Stonebreaker. Maybe someday the Japanese or Bill Gates or somebody will come up with a computer robot (Mr. Chips?) who can take attendance and make up the cafeteria list and teach children how to do the train problems and all the vital things that teachers do but in the meantime human beings have to do it and he is glad that you are willing to put your head in the noose.

As for advice to a beginner he has been racking his brain to try to come up with something helpful but all he could think of was the following:

(a) On opening day count the number of children in your class and if you have more than 20 children go right to the principal's office and tell him he has made a mistake and he cannot expect you to teach more than 20 small children at one time and do a good job.

When he gets through telling you where you can go you should ignore what he told you and go straight to the superintendent of schools instead. If he will not listen to you either you should go right to the chairman of the school board and tell him your class is too big and the principal and superintendent should be fired because they won't do anything about it.

This will establish you right off as a dedicated teacher who wants the best for her children and the school board will probably give you a big raise.

(b) If they make you teach your class anyway, even though it has 38 children and 24 of them are insane, remember not to hit the children, even in self-defense. Hitting children is illegal in many states and it is also dangerous because you never know when a lawyer might be hiding under your desk.

(c) Also never hug the children even if they surprise you and do something really nice which makes you feel like you want to hug them. Nowadays if a child goes home and tells his mother or father (or both if by some chance they actually live together) that his teacher hugged him the parent might not understand and even if the parent does understand the lawyer under your desk may not understand so either way you are safer not hugging the children.

(d) Stay out of the teachers' room at all times, especially if it does not have any windows which is usually the case. You will be depressed enough already without having to listen to the morbid conversations of experienced teachers and also you could be overcome by cottage cheese and yogurt fumes and die in there.

Seriously, schoolteaching is only about 90 percent as bad as Uncle Jack has made it out to be and he is actually glad that he was a schoolteacher for a while because it did a lot for his self-respect.

Someday when you have to quit teaching and go into some disreputable line of work like picture framing or selling timeshares in order to make a living you will be able to say, "I am not all bad. I was a schoolteacher once."

Also as long as you are a schoolteacher you can count on getting a good night's sleep every night because you will be too tired to do anything else. Uncle Jack knows.

Spelling

One of Uncle Jack's favorite subjects in grade school was spelling. He was one of those lucky people who was born with the right spelling genes so he always got "100" in spelling. For years he lived for the Friday morning spelling test when even Mrs. Stonebreaker would be forced to admit that he was not completely worthless.

Sometimes he wonders if teachers still teach spelling the way they did in the old days when they would put a list of words on the board on Monday and then beat those words to death every day until Friday when they would give the test.

This did not make a whole lot of sense to Uncle Jack because he already knew how to spell the words before Mrs. Stonebreaker even picked them out. Other kids could stare at those words for five days and use them in 25 different sentences and still misspell half of them on the test. They were the poor unfortunates who could never become writers and instead had to settle for making fortunes in real estate or whatever.

Uncle Jack has wondered how kids who were not born with the spelling gene ever survived school at all. They certainly didn't get any help from the English language which is full of words like "rough", "dough", "bough", "cough" and "through", all of which are spelled the same but pronounced differently.

Nobody has ever proved that spelling tests help kids learn how to spell but Uncle Jack knows they are a very good way to make some kids hate school and feel bad about themselves.

So that's why he wonders if they are still doing stuff like that in schools.

Yo Grads! Listen Up

Uncle Jack would like to take this opportunity to congratulate all those young persons who will graduate from high school this month. As far as he is concerned graduating from high school is one of life's crowning achievements and he only regrets that so many young men and women fall by the wayside, never to know what it means to reach the pinnacle.

For as Uncle Jack knows it is the high school graduates who become the movers and shakers, the captains of industry, the leaders in every walk of life. For them and them alone are reserved the Mercedes Benzes, the Lincoln Town Cars and the Range Rovers of the future. What it boils down to is that if you can survive high school without going completely bonkers there is probably nothing in life that can stop you from achieving your goals with the possible exception of early pregnancy.

Uncle Jack has been ruminating a lot about high school this week because he got a call from an old friend in his home town inviting him to attend the 50th annual reunion of his high school graduation class this summer. He has never gone to a high school reunion before but he has decided to go this year because his friend said it might be the last one. There were only 100 people in Uncle Jack's class to begin with and apparently they have been dropping like flies in recent years, many of them as a result of bad habits they picked up in high school such as drinking and smoking and ambition.

Anyway he has been trying to think of some good advice he could give today's high school graduates now that he has been out in the real world for half a century. Unfortunately he has not come up with anything worth mentioning except "if you haven't started smoking don't start and if you have, quit now"—but you do not have to be a high school graduate to give good advice like that.

Just about everything he could say about how to live your life has already been covered pretty well by bumper stickers such as "Save the Whales", "I'd rather be in Hatteras" and "Hug your kid today" (which he hopes you will save for later).

If you want to know the truth everything is changing so fast today that he is afraid that most of the advice he would give you would be wrong and you would wind up as poor as he is.

On the other hand if you wound up as happy as he is that would not be so bad. And he can tell you for sure that you do not have to have a lot of money to be happy and also that a lot of people who do have a lot of money are not very happy.

As far as he is concerned the best situation you can be in is to have a lot of money and be very happy at the same time but he has not figured out how to do that himself so he is not much help in that department.

Anyway Uncle Jack is very proud of each and every one of you who will receive a high school diploma this month and he hopes you will cherish it enough to want to take it to the framing shop of your choice and have it expensively matted and framed so you can be proud to hang it on the wall in your office at the **Burger King** or your cubicle in the county office building or wherever you happen to wind up working.

And if you need assistance finding a good framer Uncle Jack will be more than happy to help. He firmly believes that high school graduates should stick together.

Something is Rotten In the State of North Carolina

Uncle Jack was sitting up on his deck the other day watching the pelicans and replenishing his bodily fluids when he started smelling this really bad stench that was coming in on the wind from somewhere over on the mainland. At first he thought maybe another hog waste lagoon had let go into the Neuse River or maybe some farmers were burning wet stumps again.

Anyway Uncle Jack was not sure where the stink was coming from until he read the paper the next day and learned that the University of North Carolina athletic department is now a more-or-less wholly owned subsidiary of the Nike Shoe Company.

He got so mad when he read about this that he tore the paper into shreds and threw it in the trash so he does not have the exact figures in front of him but he can tell you that the Nike company is paying the University a huge amount of money in exchange for using Nike products exclusively in its athletic programs.

This means that UNC athletes will become running, jumping, swimming, skating, vaulting, and tackling billboards for Nike, the very same company noted for its enlightened labor practices in the sweatshops of the Far East where their obscenely expensive sneakers are assembled by obscenely underpaid young women.

Apparently the people who run the University of North Carolina do not see anything wrong with an arrangement like this. In fact a number of university officials have actually said in public how proud and happy they were that Nike chose UNC to pimp for their products instead of some other lesser institution of higher learning down the road.

If you want to know the truth Uncle Jack is not sure why he is so upset about this latest development when it is just one more step along the sordid path that too many of the country's major colleges and universities started down years ago. Big-time college athletic programs have been the hog farms of academia for such a long time now that it seems a futile gesture to point his popgun in that direction.

He does wonder, though, how young people in our colleges and universities are supposed to acquire values that will prepare them to lead exemplary lives when the colleges and universities in which they matriculate (Latin for "party") are ready to sell out to the highest bidder at the drop of a hat, or a shoe or a shirt.

What's next? The Nike swoosh mark emblazoned on the Old Well?

Make me an offer, says once-proud UNC.

Taking the Laptop Leap

Poor Gary Kasparov is not the only one who has tangled with computers lately. Uncle Jack has decided to join the 20th century before it is too late by acquiring a real computer with which he can hook up to the internet and do amazing things like write letters to his grandchildren electronically at about a hundred times the cost of regular mail.

He decided to get what they call a "laptop" computer because one of the main features of a laptop is that you can haul it around wherever you go such as out on the deck or into the living room where your barcalounger is located or into the bedroom if you are too lazy to sit in your barcalounger.

That was the easiest decision he had to make, though, because he found out there are about 200 laptop computers out there in the marketplace and they are all wonderful for various reasons, none of which Uncle Jack is capable of comprehending.

Little did he know, for example, that some laptops have 16 megabytes of RAM while others have only 8 or even 4. He has no idea what a megabyte is but more is better, apparently, which is not true of everything such as children. Nor did he know that all laptops have "hard drives" whose prowess is measured in "gigabytes" which are even better than megabytes for many purposes.

He now knows that some laptops have "floppy disks" and some have CD-ROMs and some have both and he is confident that one day he will know what they are and why they are so important.

In the meantime he is reading everything he can get his hands on about laptop computers, much of which consists of sentences like these:

"The DTK notebook uses a UMC chip set, 256K of synchronous L2 cache, and EDO DRAM."

"The 133-MHz CD PowerBrick had low benchmark test scores compared with similar machines, but a 12.1-inch active-matrix display, a 1.3GB Toshiba hard disk, a four-year warranty, and a bundled 28.8/14.4-Kbps fax modem tip the scales back in its favor."

Uncle Jack prides himself on being a high school graduate but he has to confess that his confidence has been shaken somewhat by his first encounters with "computertalk". Reading William Faulkner in Urdu would be a snap compared to what he has plowed through in the last couple of weeks. But he did finally make a decision about which laptop to buy.

He has ordered a Gateway Solo 2100 which as far as he can tell has plenty of megabytes and gigabytes and hard drives and both a floppy disk and a CD-ROM and numerous other features that might come in handy when he writes to his grandchildren such as a modem which takes the place of a stamped envelope and only costs $110.

The main reason he bought a Gateway, though, is because he could sit in his barcalounger and order it over the phone instead of driving to Virginia Beach to get it. They told him they would send it as soon as the snow melts up in South Dakota and the UPS trucks can get to the factory which could be any week now.

Uncle Jack has a sinking feeling that his life will never be the same. Pandora never knew what hit her either.

To Boldly Go....

Uncle Jack is pleased to report that this is the very first column he has written with the aid, if that is the right word, (he could have chiseled this on stone in half the time) of his brand new state-of-the-art Gateway Solo 2100 Multimedia Notebook, also known as his *&%#@! laptop. Actually he should say that this is the first paragraph he has written on his new laptop because he is not at all sure that he will make it to the end without doing something inadvertently that will cause the screen to go blank. Also he has no confidence that once he gets far enough to "save" what he has written that he will not lose it forever somewhere in the electronic labyrinth.

Nevertheless he is determined to persist and eventually prevail over this incredible machine which he knows he will never understand but which he thinks might be both useful and fun in the long run (assuming they will let him use it in the old folks home or the loony bin, whichever comes first).

He can tell you that nothing is simple with the sole exception of pushing the "on" button which you would think would also be the "off" button but this is not the case. He is not going to try to explain what you have to go through to turn the thing off but he can tell you that if Lincoln had written the Gettysburg Address on Uncle Jack's laptop he never would have gotten to the cemetery in time to deliver it.

As of this writing Uncle Jack has not yet found his way to the internet which was the main reason for getting his laptop in the first place. (He has hallucinations about becoming a major player in the lucrative world of online antique print and map sales.) Today as he hunts and pecks he is waiting for the **Sprint** man to come and install a second telephone line for his laptop which he has discovered he desperately needs, mainly because he cannot be on the internet and talk with the Gateway Computer Company's technical support staff out in South Dakota at the same time. This is one of the many hidden costs of doing business on the internet and he is sure he will discover many more before he makes his first dime, if he ever does.

So far Uncle Jack has spent perhaps four hours on the phone with three different Gateway technicians who have, with infinite patience, helped him track down and eliminate a bewildering variety of glitches including pollution of the hard drive which is a condition he urges you to avoid at all cost. While these technicians all sounded like they had escaped from the cast of **Fargo** he can tell you they know their stuff by golly.

He has to confess that notwithstanding all the frustrations and aggravations of the first couple of weeks with his new laptop he really loves it. For years he has been saying to all who would listen that computers are not for Uncle Jack—not while there are books to read and beaches to walk on. You'll never find him sitting for hours in a stuffy room, pushing a little arrow around a screen; that's for nerds who can find nothing better to do with their precious time on earth. Bill Gates will never see a dime of Uncle Jack's hard-earned money. That's what he said and it was all a lie. He is hooked.

See you on the net, folks. Watch for Uncle Jack's Web Page—coming soon to your screen at www.yellowhousegallery.com

Digital Brain Surgery

Uncle Jack's tortuous journey through cyberspace ended abruptly this week. Last Saturday morning his laptop refused to "boot up" in the normal fashion when he turned it on and after two hours of diagnostic probing by phone the computer doctor in South Dakota decided that a serious operation was needed. Uncle Jack's laptop would have to have its "hard drive" replaced immediately.

The doctor explained that this was roughly equivalent to a brain replacement in a human being and that his laptop would remember nothing after the operation. It would not remember any of the e-mail letters from potential customers all over the globe. It would remember none of the dozens of e-mail addresses in Uncle Jack's electronic address book. It would remember none of the programs Uncle Jack has installed over the past few weeks to operate his modem, his printer, his scanner and God knows what else.

When he installs his new hard drive next week Uncle Jack will resume his voyage through cyberspace from the digital equivalent of square one. Incurable optimist that he is, Uncle Jack had saved nothing onto floppy disks, a simple procedure that would have saved him hours of tedious work in days to come—a mistake he will not make again?

There was a time when Uncle Jack would have greeted this dreadful news with all manner of ranting and raving and carrying on over the unfairness of it all and he would be unfit for normal social intercourse for days. His children would have cowered in their rooms and his cats and dogs would have gone to live with the neighbors.

He is pleased to report that this is no longer the case. He is not happy about this unfortunate development but neither is he despairing. Being told that his hard drive needs replaced is not the same as being told that he has inoperable cancer of the goiter or that one of his granddaughters has eloped with a lawyer. In other words Uncle Jack has at last achieved a healthy perspective on life that allows him to distinguish between the trivial and the important. And not a moment too soon, either, his loved ones will tell you.

Anyway the demise of his hard drive has given Uncle Jack at least three whole days to read another book and Mrs. Uncle Jack has found the perfect book for him. It is called **Into Thin Air** and it is about climbing Mt. Everest, with special attention to the tragic events of May 1996 when eight people died on one expedition.

Uncle Jack has long wondered why anybody in his right mind would risk his life to climb to the top of a mountain and he is hoping this book will shed some light on this question. If you want to know the truth he doesn't really care very much about why they do it but it's a fairly short book so it's not like he is going to waste a lot of time.

He does know that while those people were dying unspeakably horrible deaths on the top of a mountain in Nepal in May 1996 Uncle Jack was spurring himself to new heights of self-indulgence by trying to drink at least one pint of Guinness in every pub in Ireland. Like the mountain climbers he failed, but at least he lived to try again another day.

And if he writes a book about it he guarantees it will have a happy ending as well as a happy middle and a happy beginning.

Never a Dull Moment

Uncle Jack is pleased to report that he and Mrs. Uncle Jack have arrived safely in Nawlins, Looziana, to the extent that it is possible to arrive safely in a place like New Orleans. Fortunately they were not walking along the Mississippi a few hours after they got here when a big freighter full of corn ran into the Hilton Hotel and a shopping mall and made a terrible mess. Fortunately nobody was killed but Uncle Jack heard that 15 lawyers were injured when they trampled each other trying to see who could be first to sue the shipping company.

Never a dull moment in Nawlins, Looziana and that's for sure.

Also there was nothing dull about the trip down here which consisted of 16 hours of white-knuckle racing down Interstates 95, 20, 85, 65 and 10, all of which are apparently provided by the taxpayers of the U.S. primarily for the convenience and profit of the American trucking industry. Most of the time Uncle Jack felt like his new pre-rusted Plymouth Voyager was the filling in a truck sandwich.

The worst part of the trip was the couple of hours on Interstate 95 in North Carolina which is the main route to and from Florida for all the drug couriers, most of whom seem to drive cars that are incapable of speeds slower than 90 mph.

Uncle Jack has been on 95 many times before so it was no surprise but he can tell you he was happy to get to Interstate 20 in South Carolina which is a road he has never taken before in his whole life.

Once he got on 20 and from then on all the way to New Orleans he was seeing Ramada Inns and

McDonalds and Wendys and Dennys that he had never seen before and he felt like a real pioneer.

Uncle Jack had never been in Alabama or Mississippi before and he didn't know what to expect but he can tell you they really know how to keep their Interstate highways looking nice. He is not sure if they can't afford billboards yet or what but it was pleasant to look at trees and flowers for a few hours after running the gauntlet of South of the Border signs on Route 95. To paraphrase one of those signs, "He never sausage a mess."

Anyway it was a long trip and Uncle Jack was very happy to see the sign that said "Welcome to New Orleans, America's Most Interesting City" even though it was full of bullet holes. Somehow the bullet holes seemed like an appropriate symbol for a city where over 400 people were murdered last year.

He was not too happy to learn that three of the most recent killings were perpetrated in a pizza parlor only two blocks from where he is living but he is inclined to look on the bright side. What are the chances that this is going to happen again anytime soon?

Also he takes comfort from a letter to the editor in the **Times-Picayune** which points out that tourists should not worry too much about getting murdered in New Orleans because 95% of the victims are actually residents of the city.

Cold comfort, that is.

Spooge

One of the things Uncle Jack likes best about spending time in a new place is learning new words and improving his vocabulary. This is especially important now that he is getting old and senile and he is forgetting a lot of the words he learned a long time ago. He would give you an example of the words he keeps forgetting but he cannot think of one right off.

Fortunately he is learning many new words in New Orleans to take the place of some of the ones he has forgotten. Many of them are very interesting, too, such as **jambalaya** and **gumbo** and **etouffee** and **roux** and **lagniappe** and he can hardly wait to get back to the Outer Banks and start to work them into conversations every chance he gets so that people will know he is a lot more sophisticated than he looks.

Most of the new words Uncle Jack has learned in New Orleans have something to do with eating and drinking which is probably not surprising considering that eating and drinking are the two major activities down here along with throwing up which runs a distant third and is pretty much limited to the college crowd.

Uncle Jack did learn one new word that he likes very much during Mardi Gras but he is not sure how often he will be able to work it into conversations because it does not come up very often outside of New Orleans. The word is **spooge** and it refers to the scummy coating that builds up on Bourbon Street after four straight nights and days of Mardi Gras activities during which it is impossible for the street cleaners to do their job because of all the bodies lying in the gutters.

As far as Uncle Jack can tell the word **spooge** is sort of a loose amalgamation of **goo** and **sponge** and is somebody's attempt to describe the indescribable mixture of spilled beer, spilled Hurricanes (a fruit juice and rum concoction which tastes a lot better going down than it does coming up, which it inevitably does), pulverized Doritos, smashed Lucky Dogs, mustard, ketchup, ice cream, pretzels—and vomit, which acts as a kind of binder.

All these ingredients are ground into a fine paste by tens of thousands of milling feet and distributed more or less evenly to a depth of perhaps one-fourth of an inch over every square foot of Bourbon Street and its sidewalks.

As soon as Fat Tuesday is over and the bodies have been hauled away the streetwashers go to work and by morning Bourbon Street is restored to its normal state of grunginess and most of the **spooge** will have found its way to the Mississippi where it joins the equally repulsive effluents of a thousand communities upstream, eventually reaching the once-pristine waters of the Gulf of Mexico. Fortunately shrimp and oysters seem to thrive on the stuff.

Anyway Mardi Gras is over for another year and Uncle Jack is not the only one who is thankful for that. He is happy to report that it was not all **spooge** and not everybody got falling down drunk and ran naked through the streets. Considering that there must have been 300,000 people in the French Quarter yesterday, most of them ingesting mind-altering substances like there would be no tomorrow, it was an amazingly peaceful day. It made Uncle Jack think that maybe there is hope for mankind after all. On second thought, naaah. You couldn't prove it by Mardi Gras.

Fat Tax

Dear Uncle Jack,

I saw some politicians on the TV the other day and they were yelling at each other about something called a "fat tax." Are they really going to put a special tax on fat people, Uncle Jack?

Pleasingly Plump
Waves

Dear Pleasingly,

Uncle Jack is happy to tell you that you heard wrong. For right now at least you do not have to worry about paying an extra tax just because you are metrically challenged. Those politicians were actually talking about a "flat tax" which he is not going to try to explain because he does not understand it himself. It must be a very good deal for rich people, though, because they are the only ones who seem to be pushing it.

Anyway Uncle Jack is not going to lose any sleep over the flat tax because he is sure there is not a fat (or flat) chance that the U.S. Congress is going to pass a flat tax in his lifetime—or even in this century, whichever comes first.

He says this because he knows that even though we have some of the finest congressmen money can buy, they are not the kind of people who rush into things. Uncle Jack will be happy if they just get a budget passed so there will be no interruption in the flow of his entitlements.

Flatly,
Uncle Jack

Football Blues

Dear Uncle Jack,

I have been happily married for almost six months to a really swell guy but now that it's football season I'm beginning to wonder if I made a mistake. All my husband does on Saturday and Sunday anymore is sit on the couch and drink beer and watch football on TV with his rowdy friends.

We used to do a lot of fun things on weekends like we would go over to Bodie Island and sit in one of the Park Service duck blinds and make believe we were in a jacuzzi in the Bahamas or we would go over to the mall and watch the seagulls drop their clams in the parking lot.

Now he won't even go out of the house on weekends and when I say something about it he tells me to bug off. To tell you the truth, Uncle Jack, I'm almost desperate enough to pack my things and go home to Mom and I would do it, too, except that she watches football all the time herself and all she ever talks about is how she would like to sack John Elway, whoever he is.

What can I do, Uncle Jack? You are my only hope.

Football Widow
Nags Head

Dear Widow,

Uncle Jack is very glad you wrote to him because he knows what you are going through and he is pretty sure he can help you. But you have to put on your thinking cap and really try to understand what he is going to tell you which you probably won't like. First of all you have to realize that it is not your husband's fault that all he wants to do on weekends is watch football on TV.

Ever since he was a tiny boy baby the various forces of society have been shaping and preparing him for the day when he would be a man and it would be time for him to take his rightful place in front of the tube.

Now that he is a man he has no choice. When he hears the voices of Terry or Big John or Dandy Don he must watch football, just like when you hear the voice that tells you it is time to clean the oven you cannot rest until the oven is clean.

You must understand that men are supposed to watch football on TV and you should be glad that your husband is a real man and not some kind of wimp who spends his weekends riding around on a golf cart.

If you can truly believe what Uncle Jack has told you so far you are well on the way toward getting through the football season and saving your marriage. All you have to do is find some constructive ways to spend your time and not bother your husband for the next few weekends.

If you can clean the oven quietly that would be a good thing to do, but stay away from the refrigerator because you could be trampled. There is something about watching football on TV that makes men very thirsty, especially for Lite Beer from Miller.

Some people will tell you to be a good sport and try to learn about football so you can sit in the living room and enjoy it with your husband and his friends. You must believe Uncle Jack when he tells you this is very bad advice. Your husband does not want you to watch football on TV with him because there are many things he would have to explain to you and it would take all the fun out of watching.

For example, he would have to explain to you why the best play in football is the one where three or four enormous men jump on the little quarterback and try to separate his head from his body. When this play is successful, as it often is, the quarterback has to be carried off the field on a stretcher and taken directly to the emergency room.

Also Uncle Jack is pretty sure your husband would not want you to see him drooling over the practically naked cheerleaders when they are bouncing around the sidelines the way they do.

The best thing for you to do is to get out of the house completely on weekends. Fall is the very best time to transplant sandspurs, for example, or you might want to get together with some of the other football widows and drive up by Moyock and watch the leaves fall off the trees.

Anyway Uncle Jack hopes he has helped you see some ways to get through football season and save your marriage, too. All it will take is a little understanding on your part.

Sagely,
Uncle Jack

Hitting the Cut-off Man

Dear Uncle Jack,

I have wanted to ask you a question about baseball for a long time but I had to wait for my husband to die, which he did, thank goodness, during a doubleheader last Saturday afternoon. If you want to know the truth he was dead for four hours before I even noticed which did not surprise me because every time he turned on the TV to watch a baseball game he would fall asleep immediately and he would not wake up again until it was over.

Needless to say I was forced to endure a lot of baseball during the 35 years we were married and my question to you is this: How could there be such a thing as insomnia in the world as long as there is baseball on TV? I would rather watch two communists play chess.

Baseball Widow
Southern Shores

Dear Widow,

Uncle Jack's heart goes out to your departed husband who must have suffered greatly during his long and unfortunate marriage to such a sarcastic person as yourself. It is fairly obvious to Uncle Jack that you have not even tried to learn enough about the great game of baseball so that you too could understand and appreciate it as much as your late husband did.

Take the spitting, for example. If you had given your husband a chance he could have opened your eyes to the wonderful world of spitting in which there is never a dull moment if you know what to watch for. He could have told you about the various types of chewing tobacco which produce the almost infinite variety of spitting styles which trained observers like Uncle Jack and your late husband could use to glean valuable information as the game proceeded.

For example, Uncle Jack can tell you almost to the minute when a manager is going to change pitchers just by the amount of tobacco juice running down his chin. And if they have a good cameraman who knows how to move in close to the cheek area Uncle Jack can tell you if the manager is working on a gob of real Red Man or just some wimp-type chew that comes in little packets like Lipton's tea and tastes like Wrigley's spearmint.

And he can tell you it makes a lot of difference over a whole season if the manager is a real man who can handle a real chew or if he is some kind of sissy who goes for one of the designer brands. This is not something you can hide from your players for very long, especially when they are sober.

And there is a lot more to baseball than just spitting, too. If you know the game you can tell what kind of underwear a pitcher is wearing just by the way he handles himself on the mound.

Anyway there is a lot more Uncle Jack could tell you about baseball if he had time such as "hitting the cut-off man" which is so important that if a player cannot learn to do it right he might as well quit baseball and go into real estate just like everybody else.

Sportingly,
Uncle Jack

Olympic Porchsitting

Lucky for Uncle Jack the Olympic Committee has not made Porchsitting into one of the official games yet because he is not too crazy about the idea of being in Atlanta at this time of the year, especially if he had to engage in serious competition with the best Porchsitters from all over the world in all that heat and humidity they have down there.

He knows it is only a matter of time before Porchsitting gets approved as an official Olympic Game because the AARP has been lobbying pretty hard for it the past couple of years and they usually get what they want.

Maybe if Uncle Jack is really lucky he will be able to compete in the summer games in Japan in the year 2000 because he has heard that they have very good beer over there and it is not so humid.

Anyway he is going to keep honing his Porchsitting skills which he feels are already world class in some areas such as Osprey Appreciation, Porpoise-spotting, Gull-feeding from the Prone Position, Pelican-counting and Synchronized Rocking (with Mrs. Uncle Jack). He needs more polishing in a few others like Avoiding Eye Contact With the Renters Next Door. (He still has a tendency to let himself be drawn into banal conversations which cause him to lose concentration and which could cost him points in international competition.)

Seriously, Uncle Jack has been trying to watch the Olympics on TV from time to time this week but he has to confess it is hard going. For one thing they have all these events which it is hard for him to believe that even the people who are competing would find them interesting, such as pommel horse riding. He knows he is bored when he starts looking forward to the next car commercial which is never more than 30 seconds away, fortunately.

Speaking of commercials Uncle Jack finds himself pining for the old days before TV when the athletes were all amateurs more-or-less and they competed against each other pretty much to see who was best instead of to see who was going to get the best shoe contract. It is hard to believe anymore that not so many years ago the great Jim Thorpe had to give up his Olympic medals because he had made a few bucks playing semi-pro baseball. That sort of thing seems downright un-American now when every member of the U.S. men's basketball team is a multi-millionaire professional player.

Ironically those filthy rich NBA stars come as close as any of the Olympic athletes to the old notion of competition for competition's sake. All that matters to them is showing the world that they are the very best at what they do.

They play for the sheer pleasure of playing and maybe a little bit for the fun of humiliating opponents from basketball hotspots like Argentina where most of the players were probably chasing cattle around the pampas until recently.

But enough pontificating. It is time for Uncle Jack to return to the porch for another gruelling practice session. When the time comes to porchsit for his country he will be ready.

He could also use a nice chair contract.

PETA

Dear Uncle Jack,

I read in the paper where some crazy people from up north are going around trying to get people to stop fishing. They say it is not fair for people to kill fish to eat and it is even worse for people to fish for "sport" which is where you get fish to bite on hooks and drag them through the water for a while and then let them go. They say the hooks hurt the fishes' mouths and it is not fair for humans to hurt fish just because they are bigger.

Is this the dumbest thing you ever heard of or what, Uncle Jack?

Skip Charter
Hatteras Village

Dear Skip,

Uncle Jack would hesitate to say this is the dumbest thing he ever heard of because he used to attend a lot of commissioners' meetings back when he was a reporter and he heard some doozies then, too.

He does have to admit, though, that when he first heard about People for the Ethical Treatment of Animals which is what they call themselves he thought maybe they were all suffering from some kind of protein deprivation or something.

He does try to give people the benefit of the doubt even when they seem like worthy objects of ridicule so he has been pondering the whole business of the food chain and man's place in it a lot lately, especially during the late evening when he is likely to be consuming only distilled vegetable matter which is not likely to offend any pressure groups with the possible exception of the WCTU if there still is one. As far as he knows there is not yet a group called People for the Ethical Treatment of Barley for which many of us can be thankful.

Anyway Uncle Jack has been reading as much as he can find about what the PETA folks say about "ethical treatment of animals" and he has to admit they make some pretty good points and he is not going to read any more because if they talked him into treating animals fairly it could really mess up his life, especially at mealtimes.

It is very hard for Uncle Jack to contemplate a life without hamburgers, hot dogs, pork chops, chicken wings, filet mignons, fish sandwiches and all the other non-vegetable stuff he eats every day. He tries not to think about where the hamburger came from or how the cow felt when she got whacked on the head with a sledgehammer or however they do it these days. (Maybe they get whacked on the head with computers.)

On the other hand Uncle Jack is not inclined to poke too much fun at people who are nice enough to try to understand how a cow or chicken or pig might feel about sacrificing his or her life to satisfy some person's craving for a Big Mac or a plate of spicy Buffalo Wings.

About fish Uncle Jack is not so sure. He does not know whether or not fish experience physical distress or even angst when pierced by a hook and dragged through the water against their presumed wills. He can tell you that at one time he thought that matching wits with a wily fish (estimated brain weight 1/4 oz.) was man's noblest sport. Now he doesn't even own a rod and reel.

But how he loves those fish sandwiches at Sam and Omie's.

Ambivalently,
Uncle Jack

Proud to be a Quitter

Most of the people who don't smoke must have a hard time understanding why smokers smoke when even the dumb smokers who never finished high school must have heard by now that smoking is bad for their health.

Some of the non-smokers probably tried to learn how to smoke when they were young but it made them sick right off the bat instead of having to wait thirty years to get lung cancer. They were lucky.

Uncle Jack does not smoke but it isn't hard for him to understand why people do smoke even though they know it makes them cough and it stinks up their clothes and it is costing them a fortune. Uncle Jack knows why they smoke because a long time ago he used to smoke, too, and he can still remember what it was like. For ten years he started every day with a cigarette and ended every day with a cigarette and in between he smoked at least twenty more, two or three of which he really enjoyed.

This is not something Uncle Jack is proud of. It is not easy to admit that he was a slave but for ten years Uncle Jack belonged to the Marlboro Man. One day Uncle Jack really got fed up with the Marlboro Man and he decided he would never smoke a cigarette again. He knows exactly when this was because it was on the very day his only begotten son was born. (Uncle Jack has always had a flair for the dramatic.)

Actually Uncle Jack had tried to quit smoking many times before but the Marlboro Man wouldn't let him. This time, though, Uncle Jack had help from Bob Newhart.

Back in the old days Bob Newhart was a stand-up comedian who did funny skits where he would pretend he was talking on the phone to somebody. In one of those skits he pretended to be a high pressure salesman in England who was talking to Sir Walter Raleigh.

Raleigh has just discovered tobacco in America and he is trying to convince this salesman that there is big money to be made in something called "cigarettes" which he tries to describe over the phone: "So you take this weed and you let it dry out and then you crumble it up and wrap it in a little paper tube," the salesman says. "O.K. Walt, baby, I follow you so far but then what?"

"You put the little tube of tobacco in your mouth and set fire to it?" he says, beginning to laugh uncontrollably. After he recovers he says, "And then what do you do, Walt?"

"You ...you...breathe the smoke into your lungs?!! Walt, baby, you've got to be kidding!!"

Anyway Uncle Jack has not smoked a cigarette since November 2, 1961 and he cannot even begin to figure out how much money he has not spent on cigarettes in that time but it must have been enough to pay for all the bourbon he has consumed in the same period. We are talking real money here.

He would like to conclude by saying that he would be happy to serve as an inspiration to anybody who would like to quit smoking. If somebody as inherently spineless as Uncle Jack can quit, he is sure that anybody can.

And if all else fails he will let you borrow his Bob Newhart record.

Workaholics

Uncle Jack read an amazing article in a magazine the other day about people called "workaholics" who like to work so much that they work all the time except when they are sleeping, and they don't sleep very much either because they would rather work than sleep.

The article said these people like to work so much they hate weekends and holidays and they think Monday is the best day of the week. Whenever their wives manage to drag them off on vacation somewhere they take along their briefcases full of work and they spend most of their time talking on the telephone instead of swimming and fishing.

You can probably see why Uncle Jack thought this was pretty amazing. He tried work himself once a long time ago and he couldn't see anything in it at all. It is very hard for him to understand why anybody would like work so much that they would want to do it all the time.

At first Uncle Jack thought this writer made the whole thing up but now he thinks maybe there might really be people like that even though he has never actually seen one.

The people Uncle Jack hangs around with are definitely not what you would call workaholics. Some of them are "fishaholics" and some of them "sportsaholics" and all of them are alcoholics but not a single one of them even comes close to being a workaholic.

The article says you should not feel sorry for people who are workaholics, though, because most of them are very happy. They really do like to work all the time and as long as nobody tries to keep them from working they are happy as clams. The trouble is that the wives of workaholics are not always happy because they feel neglected, so one way or the other they make the workaholic feel guilty about having so much fun working all the time.

Uncle Jack has noticed that very often the same thing happens to fishaholics and sportsaholics and alcoholics. They would be perfectly happy if people would leave them alone but that is not the way it usually works out.

According to the article the really worst thing about being a workaholic is that sometimes they work so hard they wear themselves out and all of a sudden they drop dead of a heart attack or something. That is a good enough reason right there for not getting mixed up with work if you ask Uncle Jack.

You can be sure he will be keeping a sharp eye out for the "10 Warning Signals" they give you in this article and at the first sign that he might be starting to become a workaholic he will head right for his rocking chair on the deck and stay there until he is sure he is out of danger.

For anybody who is reading this who is already a workaholic Uncle Jack will pass on a couple of suggestions that the article says will help you have better relations with your "loved ones," by which he thinks they probably mean your wife and children.

The article says you should volunteer to do household chores sometimes and also you should take your children jogging on weekends. The other suggestions are even dumber so Uncle Jack is not going to waste any more space on them. Besides he has been writing for fifteen minutes now and that is enough work for one day.

Out of the Closet

Dear Uncle Jack,

I was over at the laundromat the other day and I heard some guys talking about a new TV show about some woman who used to live in a closet or something. It sounded pretty stupid to me but they seemed to think it was a good show and I don't want to miss out on anything so I was wondering if you could tell me what they were talking about.

Linda Loblolly
Grandy

Dear Linda,

Uncle Jack is not what you would call an authority on TV shows because he never watches anything except **Jeopardy** and **Frasier** but he thinks he knows what show those guys were talking about. If you will pardon him for saying so a person would have to be practically brain dead not to know that they were talking about a sitcom called **Ellen**.

First of all Uncle Jack should explain that when they say that Ellen is coming out of the closet it does not mean that she was actually living in a closet before she came out. It was more like she was hiding in one except that she never was really in a closet at all. To be "in the closet" is what they used to call a "figure of speech" back when Uncle Jack studied English in high school. He is not sure what they call it now (if anything) because he has not seen any evidence lately that anybody is teaching English anymore.

Anyway now we get to the hard part where Uncle Jack has to explain that to be "in the closet" has a very special meaning these days which may be very hard for you to understand if you are not a high school graduate.

First Uncle Jack will have to tell you that some people are what they call "gay" which is another word that has a very special meaning nowadays. A "gay" person is not necessarily somebody who has just won the lottery or something nice like that although it is possible for a "gay" person to win the lottery and also be gay in the original or Biblical sense of being happy. (He did not say this would be easy.)

Nowadays the word "gay" is often used to describe persons who are attracted to other persons who are the same sex they are instead of to persons who are the opposite sex. Uncle Jack has no idea why these people are called "gay" but it is much shorter than "homosexual" which is another thing they are called and much nicer than many other things they are called. Also Uncle Jack does not know why some people are "gay" but he has read that it might have something to do with the kind of jeans their parents bought them when they were children.

Anyway for a "gay" person to "be in the closet" means that he or she does not want other people to know that he or she is "gay" and to "come out of the closet" means that you do not care anymore if they know.

As far as Uncle Jack can tell to "come out" can have different outcomes depending on who you are and what strata of society you hang around in. You could get beat up but on the other hand if you have your own sitcom you could get higher ratings and even get on **Oprah** if you come out.

Didactically,
Uncle Jack

Ashes to Ashes

Uncle Jack got a very nice letter last week asking him to join a new Mausoleum Society they are starting up over on Roanoke Island. It was very exciting for him to get this letter because he hardly ever gets asked to join anything.

The letter had a picture of their building which is very good looking and it should hold up pretty well, too, because they are going to build it out of granite instead of particle board which is what most of the new buildings around here are made of.

Anyway Uncle Jack was very interested in joining the Mausoleum Society until he found out what a mausoleum was. Now he is wondering how he got on their mailing list.

That letter did start Uncle Jack thinking about what should be done with his mortal remains when he kicks the bucket, which he hopes won't be anytime soon but one never knows.

Different people in different parts of the world have certainly come up with a lot of interesting and unusual ways to dispose of their mortal remains. Uncle Jack knows quite a lot about this because many years ago his mother-in-law gave him a subscription to **National Geographic** magazine which she must have thought would be more uplifting for him than some of the other magazines he used to read before they quit selling them at the 7-11.

It was more uplifting, too, in the long run. At first Uncle Jack would just skim through the **National Geographic** looking for pictures of topless native girls but after a while he started reading the words, too, and he learned many interesting things that way.

One thing he learned is that over in India they get rid of their mortal remains by building a big bonfire and burning them up. Another thing he learned is that Eskimos put their mortal remains on floating ice cakes and let them drift out to sea, but he is not sure if the E.P.A. lets them do that anymore.

If you want to know the truth none of these methods appeals to Uncle Jack very much. On the other hand he isn't too crazy about having his mortal remains buried in the ground either, especially around here where the water table is only about three inches down.

The mausoleum sounds a lot better because they say it is clean, dry, ventilated, above ground and permanent. It sounds a lot like being buried in a condo except for the part about "permanent." If you were looking for words to describe some of the condominiums they have built around here you surely wouldn't have too much use for "permanent."

Anyway Uncle Jack wouldn't mind if they just propped up his mortal remains in his favorite rocking chair on the deck and faced them toward the ocean. For the first few days it might be hard to tell if you were looking at Uncle Jack's mortal remains or the original Uncle Jack but eventually the seagulls would figure it out and do their thing.

He knows this solution would not appeal to everybody and he wishes the Mausoleum Society the best of luck with its membership drive.

Happy New Year

Dear Uncle Jack,

Well it's a brand new year on the Outer Banks and elsewhere. I would like to know if you are making any resolutions or predictions and if so what they are so we can look back a year from now and see how stupid they were.

Avid Reader
Stumpy Point

Dear Avid,

And a Happy New Year to you, too. Uncle Jack appreciates your expression of support as he makes his annual attempt to improve himself and also to prognosticate what the future may bring to his fellow residents of the Outer Banks so they may better prepare themselves for any eventuality.

He would be the first to admit that he has not done too well in either department in recent years but he is not the kind of person who gives up easily in the face of adversity.

He has to confess that when it comes to making resolutions he has had to set his sights fairly low the last couple of years because his will power is pretty well shot. There was a time when he could actually resolve to do very hard things like quitting smoking the way he did back in 1961 and then not smoke another cigarette—ever.

Only ten years ago he could resolve to give up drinking bourbon and then go for hours without a drop but he doesn't even pretend he can do that anymore.

Last year he gave up kale because he doesn't like kale all that much to begin with but when the kale season rolled around in November there he was, stuffing his face with kale like there was no tomorrow. Needless to say this did not do much for his self-esteem.

Uncle Jack is determined not to torture himself like that again so this year he has made a resolution that he is pretty sure he can keep no matter what, to wit: he is going to stay in New Orleans until April no matter how homesick he gets for the Outer Banks.

When he sees on the Weather Channel how a humongous northeaster is pounding the Outer Banks and he wants desperately to be there to see his neighbors' houses in South Nags Head fall into the ocean, he will remember his resolution and he will stay put in New Orleans no matter how warm and pleasant and boring it is. Unless, of course, his money runs out which is always a possibility when you are a big tipper like Uncle Jack.

If you want to know the truth Uncle Jack has not been very much better at making predictions than he has at keeping resolutions. Every year for a long time he has been predicting that during the coming year another sizeable chunk of the "goodliest land under the cope of heaven" will disappear under a layer of asphalt and he has been right every time. The fact that your average high school dropout could make the same prediction keeps him from feeling too smug.

One of these years Uncle Jack's prediction is going to be wrong, though, because Mother Nature will decide it's time to do some serious unpaving but neither he nor any other prophet of doom is smart enough to know which year that is going to be.

Let's all hope it won't be this year. The stock market crash will be bad enough.

The Demon Sex

Dear Uncle Jack,

I have been reading a lot in the papers lately about how the Town of Nags Head is agonizing over what to do about dirty movies and topless bars and other sordid things like that which are threatening our way of life here on the Outer Banks. You live in Nags Head, Uncle Jack, so what do you think they ought to do.

Kari Nation
Wanchese

Dear Kari,

This is not a subject that Uncle Jack spends a whole lot of time worrying about but he has a few thoughts that he will be happy to share with you since you asked.

For one thing he knows that people have been trying to deal with the Demon Sex for a very long time—even before there was a Bible to provide them with clear guidelines. You may not believe this but anthropologists have discovered that there were harlots roaming the earth, leading men astray, as early as the Fifth Century B.C.

Down through the centuries the good people have been trying every which way to stamp out the evil manifestations of the Demon Sex (along with his cousins the Demon Rum and the Demon Dope) but he has to be honest and tell you that it does not look like they have made very much progress so far.

It has gotten so bad that if Uncle Jack's flesh was any weaker he would be inclined to throw in the towel and let the bad people have their way with him.

But Uncle Jack remains strong in his resolve and he believes that the only way to turn the tide against the

Demon Sex is to crack down even harder on his handymen (and handywomen).

To this end he suggests that during the off-season when the town police are not so busy writing speeding tickets they should go to work rounding up all the bad people such as the harlots and the men who consort with them and the people who traffic in dirty movies and the people who watch them and they should be stripped naked and tied to a stake in front of the Nags Head Town Hall (it is not too late to add a stake to the new complex and it should not push the project over budget if the commissioners don't get conned into buying a fancy rhinestone stake from Tammi Bakker or somebody like that).

Then they should schedule regular public whippings and invite the mayors of all the towns and maybe other celebrities such as Pat Buchanan or Pat Robertson to do the honors.

Uncle Jack is fairly confident that a spectacle of this nature would draw a good crowd and would go a long way toward stamping out the Demon Sex in our communities. Whether or not parents should bring their children would be up to them but if they decide to leave them home they should be aware of what they might be watching on TV.

Anyway there is a lot more Uncle Jack could say on this subject but he has run out of space and he is probably in big enough trouble already so he is going to stop right here.

Prudently,
Uncle Jack

Babies

Dear Uncle Jack,

I read in **Parade Magazine** last Sunday that many famous actresses such as Madonna, Jodie Foster, Ursula Andress, Vanessa Redgrave and Catherine Deneuve have managed to have babies even though they don't have husbands.

How do they do that, Uncle Jack?

Incredulous
Manns Harbor

Dear Incredulous,

Uncle Jack is sorry to tell you that this is one of the areas of human knowledge in which he is not quite up to snuff. He too has read in **USA Today** about various rich and famous women who have had babies without having husbands but he does not have a clue as to how they do it.

For a long time he thought maybe it had something to do with being rich enough so you could go to some clinic in Switzerland where they knew how to do it with mudpacks or something but he was wrong about that.

Later on he read in the paper where a lot of women who were not very rich at all were having babies even though they did not have husbands so it can't have anything to do with being able to go to Switzerland.

Some of these women were actually on welfare and they were not all high school graduates so it must not have anything to do with being rich or smart.

Anyway when Uncle Jack was in school Mrs. Stonebreaker taught him that you could only have babies if you had a husband and wife who were married to each other but it sure looks like it is not that way any more.

He probably could have made up a pretty good answer to your question if he put his mind to it but he is too honest to do that so it looks like you are going to have to write to Ann Landers or Miss Manners or somebody like that who is more up-to-date on where babies come from these days.

Next time ask Uncle Jack something about sports and he will try to do better.

Evasively,
Uncle Jack

Pommes de Terre au Jus

(From Uncle Jack's Outer Banks Cookbook)

Bake one ham in a covered pan at 350 degrees until approximately one-half inch of grease has accumulated on bottom of pan.

Remove ham from pan and give to truly needy family.

Cut several new potatoes, skins on, into slices about one-half inch thick. Lay potato slices in ham grease and return pan to oven.

After 30 minutes turn potato slices over. Cook until grease has been completely absorbed by potatoes.

Serve on a bed of paper towels.

Winnebago Blues

Dear Uncle Jack,

One night last week I was racing up the Bypass to get some cough medicine for my baby but I got behind this big Winnebago with Kansas plates going 25 mph and by the time I got past them it was too late. The ABC store was closed so I had to turn around and go back to South Nags Head and explain to my baby why I couldn't get her cough medicine and she got sore and made the kids go to bed instead of watching **Jeopardy** and she pulled the plug on me, too, if you know what I mean.

Needless to say I'm disgusted and the reason I am telling you all this Uncle Jack is that I know you are the kind of person who has to get to the ABC store in a big hurry yourself sometimes so you know how I feel. I thought maybe if you published this letter it would galvanize our lawmakers into action to do something about all the slow drivers on the Bypass. I think they should pass a law that would make it a felony not to drive as fast as the law allows at all times.

Junior Johnson
South Nags Head

Dear Junior,

Uncle Jack knows exactly how you feel. He, too, has spent many an hour creeping along behind large recreational vehicles on the Bypass and wondering if he would ever get where he is going which is usually but not always the ABC store. He has to confess he does enjoy reading all those stickers they put on the back of those RVs but he wonders sometime how you could get to all those scenic and historical places such as Knott's

Berry Farm and Tarpon World all in one lifetime if you never drove over 25 mph.

He is sorry to tell you he does not think there is much the lawmakers can do about this problem so from now on maybe you should do what Uncle Jack does and plan ahead so you do not have to make so many emergency trips to the ABC store. One way to do this is to take out a home equity loan and stock up on whatever you think you will need between now and the end of the tourist season. Uncle Jack is pretty sure you can deduct the interest from your income tax so that makes it a pretty good deal if you are careful not to lose your house.

On the other hand if you live in South Nags Head you are probably going to lose your house sooner or later anyway so it might not make any difference.

Uncle Jack does not think it would be a good idea to make those Winnebagos go faster because if you ask him the only thing worse than being behind a large RV going 25 mph is to be in front of one when it is going more than 25 mph. Anyway Uncle Jack knows that all those slow-moving people with the funny license plates are the ones who make it possible for him to live on the Outer Banks all the time instead of just visiting once in a while so he is willing to put up with a slow trip to the ABC store once in a while.

Diplomatically,
Uncle Jack

The Big Apple-1

By the time this **Sentinel** hits the stands Uncle Jack and Mrs. Uncle Jack will be tooling up the Eastern Shore in their new pre-rusted Plymouth Voyager, on their way to New York City.

He is pretty excited about this trip because it has been a long time since he last visited the Big Apple and he has heard that a lot of things have changed since he was there about 15 years ago.

For one thing they have a new mayor who is a terrific crime fighter and they say he has made it possible for people to walk around the streets up there without having to worry so much about getting mugged all the time.

The last time he went to New York City Uncle Jack was so worried about getting robbed that he carried his money in his shoes and he can tell you that is really hard on your feet. He still has scars on his feet from where the quarters and nickels dug in the day he tried to cover the whole Metropolitan Museum of Art in two hours.

This time he is going to carry his money in the inside secret pocket of the Antarctic Explorer parka he got from one of those mail-order companies that specializes in selling rugged outdoor clothing to indoor wimps like Uncle Jack.

He only hopes he can find his money fast enough when he needs it like when he goes into a restaurant. He has seen the "Soup Nazi" on **Seinfeld** so he knows how mad those New York restaurant owners get when you waste their time.

The last time he was in New York City he met some very nice ladies who were standing on the corner near his hotel. He is not sure if they were waiting for a bus or what but if it was a bus it must not have come very often because it seemed like those ladies were out on that corner an awful lot.

Anyway they must have known that Uncle Jack was from out of town because they kept inviting him up to their place and he would have gone, too, except that his feet hurt so much from walking around on his money. He does not expect to see them on this trip because he is sure their bus must have come by now.

Uncle Jack is trying to save enough money to go back to Ireland next spring and resume his heroic effort to drink a pint of Guinness in every pub in the country so he is going to drive to New York City instead of flying. He will be driving up Route 13 on the Eastern Shore which he remembers being sort of like a flat Blue Ridge Parkway with stoplights.

One of his favorite restaurants outside of New Orleans is over on Route 13 in Virginia and he hopes it is still there. It is called **Stuckey's** and you can't miss it because they start their billboards back around Miami, Florida and they have one about every mile except when you get into Virginia they are about every 50 feet until you get there. It's not a fancy place so Uncle Jack feels right at home there and if your taste runs to pecan logs for lunch you can't find a better place to eat between Nags Head and New York City.

Anyway he is really looking forward to seeing New York City again after all these years and if he survives he will say some more about it next week. There is always a chance that he could see somebody famous like Regis Philbin walking down the street and that would surely be worth writing about.

The Big Apple-2

Uncle Jack is pleased to report that he got to New York and back in one piece and he had a very good time, too. Everything he has heard about how the new mayor has cleaned up the city turned out to be true. New York is much nicer than it was the last time he was up there because the muggers have all moved to Raleigh or someplace and you do not have to carry your money in your shoes anymore.

If you want to know the truth, though, it might be better if you had to carry your money in your shoes because you would not be able to spend it quite as fast. He went to three plays while he was up there and it cost almost as much for the tickets as it did to send his children through college. They were good plays, though, and he probably got as much out of them as his children did out of college.

The first play he saw was called **Gross Indecency** and it was about this famous writer named Oscar Wilde who lived in England about a hundred years ago. You can tell he was a good writer because some of his books got made into movies. This did not do him a whole lot of good though because he was dead by the time they came out.

The reason he died was because he had to go to prison for a couple of years and he did not take to prison life at all. He got really sick while he was in there and they did not have penicillin or Maalox or anything in those days so he never really recovered.

The reason he had to go to prison was because he got caught doing naughty things which Uncle Jack cannot tell about in a family newspaper. Before you go rushing up there to see it, though, he has to warn you that if you are not a high school graduate you are probably going to be disappointed. Even Uncle Jack did not understand what they were talking about most of the time and that is probably a good thing. He is getting too old to learn anything new in that area.

Anyway the second play he saw was called **Mere Mortals** and he can tell you it was terrific. It was about these two mayflies who fall in love which would not be a problem except that mayflies only live for a few hours which does not give them much time to get married and have children and go to Disney World and all the other things that people who fall in love wind up doing eventually.

Anyway it was very funny but it also made you think because when it comes right down to it people do not live a whole lot longer than mayflies which they usually do not realize until it is too late. As far as he could figure out the moral of the story was if you have been thinking about going to Disney World or whatever and you haven't done it yet you better get going.

The third play he went to is the longest running play in the history of New York City which has been going for about 25 years now. It is called **Cats** and all Uncle Jack can say is there must be a lot of cat lovers in New York because he does not know who else would be crazy enough to shell out $75 to watch a bunch of people dance around in cat suits. He suggests if you want to see cats jumping around just go over to the dumpsters behind the Seamark where you can watch the real thing and it doesn't cost a dime.

There is a lot more Uncle Jack would like to say about his trip to New York City but he has run out of space and time and those are serious things to run out of.

The Law is an Ass

Dear Uncle Jack,

I am writing to you because you are one of the most prominent beer drinkers around here and I was hoping you could help me with my problem. I am 20 years old, happily married and the father of two fairly normal children. I am a high school graduate like yourself and I also matriculated to college over in Elizabeth City where I majored in heating and air conditioning.

For over a year now I have had this terrific job installing heat pumps for one of the most prestigious plumbing companies in Dare County and I am not bragging when I tell you I have not had any trouble making the payments on my new Lamborghini Countach.

Well everything was going fine and I was happy as a clam until about three weeks ago when they passed the new law that you have to be 21 years old before you can drink beer anymore. Now I have a real problem because whenever I spend a whole day up in some hot attic installing a heat pump I lose a lot of my vital bodily fluids by sweating and you know as well as I do that there is only one beverage that can restore your system to the proper balance at the end of a work day and it definitely is not Diet Pepsi.

Before they passed that new law I could go right home after work and get a Rolling Rock or two out of the fridge and sit in the living room surrounded by my happy little family while we all watched Sesame Street and I restored the various essential nutrients to my depleted body. But now that I can't buy my own beer anymore everything has changed. I have to depend on my mother-in-law to get it because she is the only one in our house who is over 21. The trouble is she always "forgets" to buy beer when she goes to the store and I don't know if it is because she is senile or if she is still mad at me for making her a grandmother at the age of 39.

Needless to say this beer law is making a nervous wreck out of me and I am thinking about switching over to marijuana or something. At least the people who sell that stuff don't keep asking to see your I.D. all the time.

Anyway I would like to know what you think about this beer law, Uncle Jack, and maybe you can explain why they passed such a stupid law in the first place.

Tormented at Twenty
Kill Devil Hills

Dear Tormented,

Uncle Jack cannot really tell you what he thinks about that cruel and unjust law because they would have to arrest him if he used all the words he would need to describe how he feels about it. If you want to know the truth, though, he thinks that new law is an insult to every high school graduate in N.C. who is under the age of 21. If a high school graduate cannot be trusted to consume Nature's most perfect food wisely and in moderation then Uncle Jack has to wonder what good is all the heartache and struggle of high school anyway.

He would like to suggest that if you ever want to get rid of your mother-in-law you could always turn her in to the police next time she remembers to buy beer for you. Sweet are the uses of adversity.

Machiavellially,
Uncle Jack

Shuckin' and Jivin'

Dear Uncle Jack,

I was watching **Entertainment Tonight** and they were talking about this rich and famous artist named Andy Warhol. They said he got rich and famous for painting pictures of Brillo boxes and Campbell Soup cans and then he spent the rest of his life going to parties.

I got fairly excited when I heard that because I have spent the last ten years going back and forth between shucking scallops and welfare and to be perfectly honest I have not found this to be a very rewarding life style. I would much rather be rich and famous the way Andy Warhol was so I was hoping you could tell me something I could paint pictures of that would get me out of this rut.

Jasper Jones
Wanchese

Dear Jasper,

Uncle Jack hates to be the bearer of bad tidings but he can tell you it is not as easy as it sounds to get rich and famous the way Andy Warhol did. For one thing you have to move to New York City.

There is no way you are going to get anywhere painting Brillo boxes or anything else unless you move to New York City because that is the only place you will find anybody to buy them. They have a lot of people up there who have so much money they do not know what to do with it so that is why the market for pictures of soup cans is so much better up there than it is in Wanchese or even Elizabeth City.

Uncle Jack happens to know that Andy Warhol was born in McKeesport, Pennsylvania which is a mill town where the general taste in art tends to lean toward what you would find on the Acme Auto Parts calendar. If Andy Warhol had tried to sell his pictures of soup cans in McKeesport those steelworkers would have taken him down and held his head under the Monongahela River so he did the smart thing and took his pictures up to New York City.

Unfortunately Uncle Jack has to warn you that just because you move to NYC does not necessarily mean that you will get rich and famous like Andy Warhol.They already have a million artists up there painting pictures of everything from American flags to dog-doo and most of them have to wait on tables when they are not on unemployment. Uncle Jack can tell you if he had to choose between shucking scallops in Wanchese and waiting tables in NYC it would not be hard.

He has to admit that once Andy Warhol got rich and famous he surely did have an interesting life style and also many unusual friends of which only one ever tried to kill him as far as he knows.

If you want to give it a try you will go with Uncle Jack's blessing but he prefers to stay here with his Acme Auto Parts catalog with the picture of Miss April who is wearing only one hubcap if you know what he means. If you ask him there is much to be said for life in the slow lane.

Esthetically,
Uncle Jack

The Good Old Days

Dear Uncle Jack,

You mentioned once that you first came to the Outer Banks in 1969 or thereabouts. Did you wash up in a shipwreck or what? What was it like around here in the old days?

Jenny Ecks
Colington Harbour

Dear Jenny,

Your questions have thrown Uncle Jack into a veritable fit of nostalgia. He did indeed discover the Outer Banks in 1969 and for him it gave new meaning to the old saw that life begins at 40.

He did not wash up on the beach but that might have been preferable to running the gauntlet of hog farms that used to line the highway in Currituck County before Progress hit and turned it into a fifty-mile long strip shopping center and billboard arcade.

Uncle Jack will never forget the first time he crossed the old two-lane Wright Memorial Bridge and saw Roanoke Sound and Jockey's Ridge for the first time. The view is still breathtaking and so is the traffic.

Turning south on the "Bypass" in 1969 he drove for miles before he saw a building. He can't remember what building it was and he would never be able to find it anyway now that the Bypass no longer bypasses anything.

His destination was the First Colony Inn on the oceanfront near the 13 milepost. Today he would have to look for it between the highways at the 16 milepost and how it got there is an amazing story.

He bought groceries at Harris's Grocery, now a rib joint, just down the street from the post office, now the unemployment office, and he bought fish from Midgett's Seafood, now defunct, just down the street from Austin's gas station, now Austin's Seafood. "Plus ca change, plus la meme chose" as they say in gay Paris—and straight Paris, too, for that matter.

He bought beer at Bell's store, now a Mexican restaurant, just down the street from the Foosball Palace, now eight upscale rental houses, and a short walk from the magnificent Old Nagsheader Hotel, now eight more upscale rental houses.

For essential supplies like duct tape and flyscreen he drove to Virginia Dare Hardware in Kitty Hawk, now an upscale eatery with cool jazz on Wednesday nights but not a can of WD-40 in the place.

He walked his dogs in the vast, empty Epstein Tract, now the Village at Nags Head complete with 18-hole golf course and upwards of 500 upscale rental houses cluttering the dunes.

He is happy to report that some things haven't changed a bit. He still buys his spiritual beverages at the same old ABC store on the Bypass and the fish sandwiches at Sam and Omie's still taste as good as they did in 1969, and most of those grand old cottages on the Beach Road in Nags Head are still there, even though most of them have been moved back from the ocean again since then.

Ah yes, the ocean. It's still there, too, and it hasn't changed at all. He can still sit and stare at the ocean for hours and it's 1969 all over again.

Myopically,
Uncle Jack

Afterword

Uncle Jack had this page left over so he thought he would use it to put in a plug for his quaint little art gallery and framing shop by the sea in Nags Head, North Carolina. It is called **Yellowhouse Gallery** because it is in an old yellow cottage on the beach road that was built in 1935. If he says so himself it is one of the most interesting shops on the Outer Banks and he hopes you will come and see for yourself.

For one thing he has one of the largest collections of genuine, original antique prints and maps in North Carolina. He has old charts of the Outer Banks going back to 1850 along with hundreds of Civil War battle maps and wood engravings of battle scenes.

Also he has old maps and views of cities and countries all over the world and old etchings, lithographs and engravings dealing with just about any topic imaginable, including birds, animals, fish, flowers, people, professions and trades, colleges and universities, and much more. He is proudest of his collection of wood engravings by Winslow Homer and Thomas Nast.

Yellowhouse is also chock-full of souvenir prints, posters and maps of the Outer Banks—lighthouses, beach scenes, and other views by fine local artists. A wide assortment of decorative prints and posters rounds out the collection

Uncle Jack hopes you will find time to come and visit his gallery while you are in Nags Head. In the meantime if you have access to the internet you can visit at www.yellowhousegallery.com which is linked to his other website. Y'all come, hear?

How to Order

To obtain additional copies of **Uncle Jack's Outer Banks** please write to **Yellowhouse Gallery,** P.O. Box 554, Nags Head, North Carolina, 27959. Enclose check or money order in the amount of $4.95 per copy. Please add $1.00 per copy for shipping and handling of up to five copies mailed to one address. Orders of five or more copies will be mailed to one address for a flat fee of $5.00.

To order by phone call **Yellowhouse Gallery** at (252) 441-6928. **Visa** or **Mastercard** accepted.

E-mail orders will also be accepted but security of buyers' credit card information cannot be guaranteed. Uncle Jack's address is yelnag@pinn.net

A trade discount is available for qualified buyers wishing to purchase books for resale. Please call or write for information.